lonely planet

T0031845

Great Lakes &
Midwest's

NATIONAL PARKS

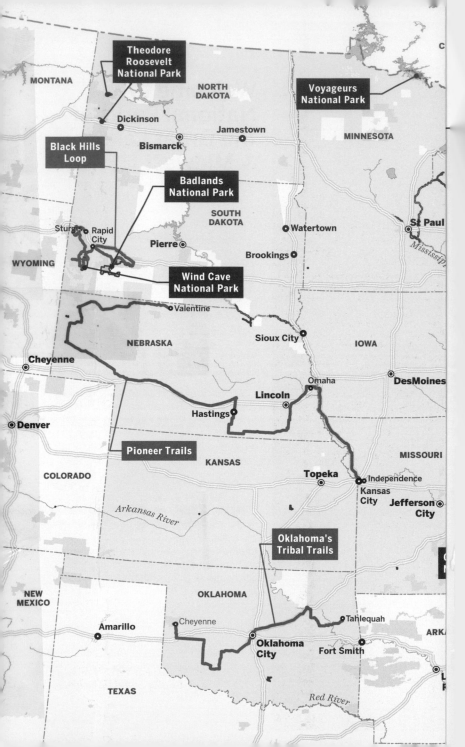

COVID-19

We have re-checked every business in this book before publication to ensure that it is still open after the COVID-19 outbreak. However, the economic and social impacts of COVID-19 will continue to be felt long after the outbreak has been contained, and many businesses, services and events referenced in this guide may experience ongoing restrictions. Some businesses may be temporarily closed, have changed their opening hours and services, or require bookings; some unfortunately could have closed permanently. We suggest you check with venues before visiting for the latest information.

Left: Boundary Waters of Minnesota; Above: Black-tailed deer at Theodore Roosevelt National Park

Plan Your Trip

Great Lakes & Midwest's National Parks Top 9

BILL CHIZEK/SHUTTERSTOCK ©

Scenic Drive, Badlands

The Badlands Loop Road (aka SD 240) is the gateway to geologic wonders (p40). Whether you go by car or bicycle, you'll pass landscapes bearing 300 million years of history as you wind past wind-sculpted spires, striated buttes and multi-hued canyons. You'll also have opportunities to get out of the car at overlooks and on nature trails – the perfect setting for immersing yourself in this often surreal, otherworldly landscape.

Wildlife Watching, Isle Royale

Whether you're staying at the Rock Harbor Lodge or out for a multi-day hiking trip, opportunities to see wildlife abound. You can sit quietly by ponds looking for signs of beavers at work or watch birds of prey soar over the clear waters. Lucky visitors might spy a moose crashing through the undergrowth or even a wolf on the prowl.

Top: Rock Harbor, Isle Royale (p70)

2

DOUGLAS SACHA/GETTY IMAGES ©

Cycling the Towpath Trail, Cuyahoga Valley

Hire a bike and go for a spin along the historic Ohio & Erie Canal Towpath, where mules once trod as they pulled boats along the old waterway. Some 20 miles of the trail pass through the national park (p46), though you can also keep going another 60 miles south, all the way to Zoarville. The wide, wooded greenway is also popular for trail running, bird-watching and horse riding.

Achenbach Trail, Theodore Roosevelt

This long, rewarding trail in Theodore Roosevelt National Park (p76) takes you through a stunning landscape of canyons, rocky plateaus and wind-swept overlooks. You'll have two river crossings and some steep ascents on this 18-mile hike, which you can complete in one long day or on a two-day outing with an overnight in the wilderness. Along the way, keep an eye out for bison, elk and pronghorn.

Island Hopping, Voyageurs

Leave the mainland behind as you hop into your canoe and paddle across the watery wilderness of northern Minnesota (p80) . You can spend your days canoeing across crystal-clear lakes and your nights camping on forested islands. It's easy to reconnect with nature at this remote park, whether camping, hiking, stargazing or just relaxing by the edge of the rocky shoreline.

Spelunking, Wind Cave

Tighten your kneepads and strap on your helmet as you plunge deep into stalactite-filled chambers lurking beneath South Dakota's Black Hills (p82). On a four-hour tour through aptly named Wind Cave, you'll crawl through narrow tunnels and clamber up rocky passageways, enjoying some stunning formations throughout the excursion. This small group tour will leave you sore but exhilarated after visiting subterranean wonders that few will ever see.

LUCIAN PROVINES/GETTY IMAGES ©

Swimming, Indiana Dunes

After clambering up the tall dunes on Lake Michigan's south shore, there's no better way to cool off than a refreshing swim in the ocean-like expanse fronting the national park (p92). There are miles of beaches to choose from. After frolicking in the waves, you can relax on the shoreline while plotting your next adventure: cycling the Praire-Duneland Trail, bird watching on the Cowles Bog Trail or learning about early settlers at the Bailly Homestead.

Sunset, Gateway Arch

It's well worth the mildly claustrophobic ride to the top of the Arch (p52) for one of the best views in the Midwest. At sunset, you can watch the sky fill with auburn shades (conditions permitting) as the the first lights of St Louis flicker across the urban landscape. Early risers can also enjoy the view from ground level with fine vantage points of the Arch at sunrise.

NAGEL PHOTOGRAPHY/SHUTTERSTOCK ©

ARCHITECT EERO SAARINEN. IMAGE: SEAN PAVONE/SHUTTERSTOCK ©

ZAKZEINERT/SHUTTERSTOCK ©

Maltese Cross Cabin, Theodore Roosevelt

Walk in the footsteps of the great conservationist who helped safeguard millions of acres of North American wilderness for future generations (p76). You can see a painstaking reconstruction of the original log cabin where Roosevelt came as a young man and learn about his transformation into an outdoors lover. The landscapes that captivated him later proved instrumental to his success as a president.

Plan Your Trip
Need to Know

When to Go

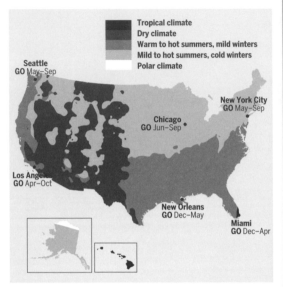

Tropical climate
Dry climate
Warm to hot summers, mild winters
Mild to hot summers, cold winters
Polar climate

Seattle
GO May–Sep

New York City
GO May–Sep

Chicago
GO Jun–Sep

Los Angeles
GO Apr–Oct

New Orleans
GO Dec–May

Miami
GO Dec–Apr

High Season (Jun–early Sep)

- Best for outdoor activities. Expect summer crowds; hit the trails early for more tranquility.

- Reserve hotels and campsites months ahead.

Shoulder (April, May & mid-Sep–Oct)

- See spring blooms in the meadows and on the hills.

- Autumn brings fiery colors and leaf-peeping crowds.

- April and May are still cold in northern states, so prepare for the elements (including possible snow).

Low Season (Nov–Mar)

- Forested paths become cross-country ski trails in winter. Ungroomed trails are ideal for snowshoeing.

- Some parks close for the season. Be mindful of ice and wintery conditions on roads and trails.

Entry Fees

Seven-day pass from free to per vehicle/pedestrian $30/15.

America the Beautiful Annual Pass

Per vehicle $80. Valid for all national parks for 12 months from purchase. Buy through National Park Service (📞888-275-8747, ext 1; www. nps.gov).

ATMs

Widely available in gateway towns.

Credit Cards

Major credit cards widely accepted; Forest Service, BLM and other campgrounds accept cash and/or checks only.

Cell Phones

Coverage inside parks is spotty at best.

Wi-fi

Some park lodges have wireless. Outside the parks, most cafes and hotels offer free wireless. Chain hotels sometimes charge.

Tipping

Tip restaurant servers 15–20%; porters $2 per bag; hotel maids $2 to $5 per night.

Advance Planning

o **Twelve months before** Reserve campsites and historic lodge accommodations.

o **Six months before** Reserve hotel rooms in satellite towns if visiting in summer. Book flights. Start training if planning to backpack.

o **One month before** Secure rental car. Take your own vehicle in for a safety inspection and tune-up if planning a long drive.

Useful Websites

Lonely Planet (www.lonelyplanet.com/usa) Destination information, travel articles, reviews.
National Park Service (NPS; www.nps.gov) Gateway to all US national parks.

Accommodations

o **Campsites** Reservation campsites as well as non-reservable backcountry camping is available. Flush toilets are common, hot showers are not.

o **Park Lodges** Well-placed lodges and cabins range from rustic to comfortable.

o **B&Bs** Available in gateway towns outside parks; often excellent and usually include wi-fi.

o **Hotels** Found in gateway towns. The best have excellent amenities and views of the water or dramatic landscapes.

Arriving at a National Park

o **Information** Pick up a park newspaper at the entry and hang onto it; they're packed with useful information.

o **Camping** If you're planning on using a first-come, first-served site, head straight to the campground. Arrive no later than mid-morning.

Daily Costs

Budget: Less than $150

o Camping & RV sites: $30–50

o Park entrance fee: free–$30

o Cheap self-catering food or cafe/diner meal: $8–20

Midrange: $150–250

o Double room in midrange hotel: $120–200

o Popular restaurant dinner for two: $50–80

o Car hire per day: from $45

Top End: More than $250

o Double room in top-end hotel: from $200

o Dinner in top restaurant: $60–100

o **Parking** People not spending the night inside a park will find parking difficult. Arrive early.

o **Visitor Centers** Best places to start exploring the parks. Purchase books and maps, ask rangers questions, check weather reports and trail and road conditions.

Getting Around

o **Car** Most convenient way to travel between the parks. Some park roads are gravel. Traffic inside parks can be horrendous.

o **Bicycles** Some parks have rentals. Good for getting around developed areas. Elsewhere, roads can be narrow.

o **Canoes & Boats** The best way to get around some areas like Voyageurs and the Boundary Waters.

Plan Your Trip
Month by Month

RAFSUN MASHRAKY/GETTY IMAGES ©

January

Strap on your snowshoes or cross-country skis and enjoy the white winter magic in Voyageurs, Badlands and Theodore Roosevelt. Kids will enjoy sledding at Sleeping Bear Dunes.

⚡ Snowshoeing

Leave the crowds behind and take to the trails of the national parks with snowshoes or cross-country skis. Seeing the parks when they're blanketed in snow is a magical experience. Rangers at some of the parks even host guided snowshoe hikes.

March

Though spring officially arrives in March, the Great Lakes do things differently, with cold and snowy days the further north you go. It's still a great month for snowshoeing and cross-country skiing.

🎊 St Patrick's Day

Downtown St Louis hosts one of the best St Patrick's Day parades in the country,

with floats, marching bands and oversized balloons. Kick things off with the 5-mile St Patrick's Day run through downtown.

April

Wildflowers start to appear in southern parks, especially around the Ozarks. Grab your binoculars and watch the spring migration, when millions of birds make the north-bound journey.

🎊 National Park Week

For one week in April, national parks host special programs and events. Early in the year, the US president announces when National Park Week will take place. On the first day of NP Week, all US parks offer free admission.

May

Visitors trickle back into Isle Royale and other northern parks. At other places, it's a great time for outdoor activities, with pleasant temperatures, blossoms on the trees and smaller crowds than summer.

◉ Spring Wildflowers

Wildflowers put on dazzling springtime displays, especially on trails at Badlands, Wind Cave, Cuyahoga Valley (pictured top left) and Indiana Dunes. Check the NPS websites for wildflower walks, talks and celebrations.

June

It's still possible to beat summer crowds in early June, though you'll need to hit the road early in the day. By late June, the parks are jammed.

☆ Falls Downtown Fridays

Just outside the national park, downtown Cuyahoga Falls hosts a family-friendly line-up of live music, local food vendors, craft beer and activities. It happens every Friday from mid-June to mid-August.

July

Steamy summer days are here, meaning it's time to cool off in the water. Make sure you include some time on the beach at Indiana

★ Best Events

National Park Week, April

Spring Wildflowers, May

Port Oneida Fair, August

Outdoor Adventure Festival, September

Foliage Season, October

Dunes, Sleeping Bear Dunes or other parks bordering the lake.

✴ Independence Day

Wherever you roam, you won't be far from a big fireworks show on July 4. A fantastic place to be is St Louis, where you can watch the night sky light up above Gateway Arch.

✴ Family Fun Days

Cuyahoga Valley hosts free family activities starting in July. Take part in hands-on art making, guided walks, fishing excursions and field games.

August

It's the height of summer, it's blazing hot, and every hotel and campsite is reserved. First-come, first-served campgrounds are your best bet.

♣ Port Oneida Fair

One weekend in August, Sleeping Bear Dunes rolls back the clock to the pioneer days with basket weaving, candle making, butter churning and more. There's live music, story-telling, lumberjack displays and wagon rides, across six historic farmsteads in Port Oneida.

September

The crowds begin to thin. If you don't mind brisk evenings, this is a beautiful time to visit the parks. Leaf-peeping begins in mid-September at northern parks like Voyageurs.

♣ Outdoor Adventure Festival

Over one weekend in September (typically the weekend after Labor Day), Everyone gets active at Indiana Dunes, with hiking, paddling, biking, bird-watching, geocaching and nature photography. This free event is inclusive, with activities for all ages and levels, including visitors with limited mobility.

♣ Big Muddy Blues Festival

St Louis celebrates its favorite rhythms over the Labor Day weekend. Most years, the festival features all local musicians playing on three riverfront stages at Laclede's Landing.

♣ Dakota Nights Astronomy Festival

Join astronomers and other star lovers on guided viewings of the night sky at Theodore Roosevelt National Park during this three-day event. By day, there are kids crafts, sun viewing (through solar scopes), special talks and planetary-themed hikes.

October

An enchanting time to travel the Great Lakes and the Midwest, October brings fiery autumn blazes to the trails and scenic drives.

☉ Foliage Season

Witness Mother Nature at her most ostentatious. The trees take on shades of red, gold and amber. The colors around the region are dazzling, especially as they blanket the forests of Cuyahoga Valley, Isle Royale, Voyageurs and anywhere around the lakeshore.

☆ Towpath Marathon

Join 1200 runners on the forest-lined Ohio & Erie Canal Towpath through the Cuyahoga Valley. If you prefer not to run 26.2 miles, try the half-marathon or a 10km run. Festivities surround the weekend race.

November

Winter creeps in quickly, with snow a possibility in many parks of the Great Lakes. Isle Royale closes for the season. Crowd-free trails make for memorable hikes.

☉ Northern Lights

Plan a wintertime visit to Voyageurs (pictured p17), the Boundary Waters or other northern parks for the best chance to see the Aurora Borealis, that shimmering wall of eerie light that stretches across the horizon. There's no guarantee you'll see them, though chances increase from fall through spring, with more frequent appearances in winter.

December

By this month winter is well under way in the parks. Some access roads and park sectors close, and visitor center and business hours are reduced. Think snowshoeing and cross-country skiing.

☉National Audubon Society Christmas Bird Count

Every year around Christmas, thousands of people take to the wilds to look for and record birds for the Audubon Society's annual survey. Many of the parks organize a count and rely on volunteers to help. Check the NPS websites for information.

Plan Your Trip
Get Inspired

PAUL HEIN/GETTY IMAGES ©

Lake Michigan

Read

- **O Pioneers!** (1913) Willa Cather's masterpiece about life on the frontier.

- **The Naturalist** (2016) Darrin Lunde's portrait of Theodore Roosevelt shows how the natural world captivated the future president who became a titan of the conservation movement.

- **Bury My Heart at Wounded Knee** (1970) Dee Brown's classic relates the battles, massacres and broken treaties that decimated Native peoples in the 19th century.

- **The Living Great Lakes** (2003) Jerry Dennis weaves together adventure, travel and natural history in this fascinating portrait of North America's inland seas.

Watch

- **Nomadland** (2020) The Badlands star in this award-winning film about modern-day nomads living on the margins of society.

- **Dances with Wolves** (1990) Acclaimed movie about the plight of Native Americans on the frontier.

- **Shifting Sands** (2016) Documentary about biodiversity in the Indiana Dunes (pictured) and ongoing ecological threats.

- **Superior** (2015) Indie film set in 1969 about two friends on an epic cycling adventure around Lake Superior.

- **Abandoned: Angelique's Isle** (2018) Story of survival after a couple is abandoned on Isle Royale in 1845.

Listen

- **Fathers & Sons** (1969) Blues classic that was Muddy Waters' biggest seller.

- **What's Going on?** (1971) A masterpiece of soulful social commentary by Marvin Gaye.

- **Highway 61 Revisited** (1965) Minnesota native Bob Dylan lays down hard-driving grooves on this poetic, bluesy album.

- **Aretha Now** (1968) Soulful hits by Motown legend Aretha Franklin.

- **Born Ready** (2020) The anthemic songs of Sicangu Lakota rapper Frank Waln address racism, oppression and social justice.

Plan Your Trip
Health & Safety

NEWCASTLE/SHUTTERSTOCK ©

Before You Go

If you require medications, bring them in their original, labeled containers. Bring a signed and dated letter from your physician describing your medical conditions and medications, including generic names. If carrying syringes or needles, be sure to have a physician's letter documenting their necessity. Some of the walks in this book are physically demanding and most require reasonable fitness. Even with the easy or easy-moderate walks, it pays to be relatively fit, rather than launch straight into them after months of sedentary living. If you're aiming for the demanding walks, fitness is essential. If you are concerned about your health in any way, have a full checkup before you start walking.

In the Parks

Visiting city dwellers will need to keep their wits about them in order to minimize the chances of suffering an avoidable accident or tragedy. Dress appropriately, tell people where you are going and respect your limitations and, above all, the wilderness and its inherent dangers. Lock valuables in the trunk of your vehicle, especially if you're parking it at a trailhead overnight, and never leave anything worth stealing in your tent.

Environmental Hazards

o **Poisonous Plants** Poison ivy is widely present in the parks. Learn to recognize its three-leaf pattern. Vines may not be easy to identify, and should be avoided.

o **Ticks** Wear long sleeves and pants to protect from ticks. Always check your body for ticks after walking through high grass or thickly forested areas. If ticks are found unattached, they can simply be brushed off. If a tick is found attached, press down around the tick's head with tweezers, grab the head and gently pull upward – do not twist it. (If no tweezers are available, use your fingers.) Don't douse an attached tick with oil, alcohol or petroleum jelly. Tick-borne diseases, like Lyme disease, is an increasing worry. If you become ill after receiving the bite, seek medical treatment immediately. Tick bites can occur any time of year, though infections are more common in warm weather.

o **Venomous snakes** There are several venomous snakes in the region, including rattlesnakes. These snakes are generally not aggressive and prefer to avoid humans. Most bites occur from people stepping on an unnoticed snake. Those bitten experience local pain and swelling. Death is rare.

Hypothermia

This life-threatening condition occurs when prolonged exposure to cold thwarts the body's ability to maintain its core temperature. Hypothermia is a real danger, regardless of the season. Cold, wet and wind can form a deadly combination, even with temperatures in the 50°Fs (10°C to 15°C). At higher elevations, hypothermia can even occur in summer. Symptoms include uncontrolled shivering, poor muscle control and irrational behavior. Treat symptoms by putting on dry clothing, giving warm fluids and warming the victim through direct body contact with another person. Prevention is the best strategy: dress in layers and wear a waterproof, windproof outer jacket.

Walk Safety – Basic Rules

o Allow plenty of time to accomplish a walk before dark, particularly when daylight hours are shorter.

o Study the route carefully before setting out. Monitor your progress during the day against the time estimated for the walk.

o Don't walk alone. Always leave details of your intended route, number of people in your group and expected return time with

★ Water Purification

To ensure you are getting safe, clean drinking water in the backcountry you have three basic options:

Boiling Water is considered safe to drink if it has been boiled for at least a minute. This is best done when you set up your camp and stove in the evening.

Chemical Purification There are two types of chemical additives that will purify water: chlorine or iodine. You can choose from various products on the market. Read the instructions carefully first, be aware of expiration dates.

Filtration Mobile devices can pump water through microscopic filters and take out potentially harmful organisms. If carrying a filter, take care it doesn't get damaged in transit, read the instructions carefully and always filter the cleanest water you can find.

someone responsible before you set off, and let that person know when you return.

o Before setting off, make sure you have a map, compass and whistle, and that you know the weather forecast for the area for the next 24 hours. Always carry extra clothing and emergency high-energy food.

Rescue & Evacuation

If someone in your group is injured or falls ill and can't move, leave one person with them while another one or more goes for help. They should take clear written details of the location and condition of the victim, and of helicopter landing conditions. If there are only two of you, leave the injured person with as much warm clothing, food and water as it's sensible to spare, plus the whistle and torch. Mark the position with something conspicuous.

Plan Your Trip
Clothing & Equipment

STEVEN SCHREMP/SHUTTERSTOCK ©

Voyageurs National Park (p80)

Deciding what gear is essential and what will weigh you down is an art. Smartphone apps, new filtration systems and battery chargers are changing the game. Don't forget essentials, but be ruthless when packing, since every ounce counts when you're lugging your gear up craggy ridges in the Badlands or portaging along marshy trails in Voyageurs.

Layering

The secret to comfortable walking is to wear several layers of light clothing, which you can easily take off or put on as you warm up or cool down. Most walkers use three main layers: a base layer next to the skin, an insulating layer, and an outer-shell layer for protection from wind, rain and snow.

For the upper body, the base layer is typically a shirt of synthetic material that wicks moisture away from the body and reduces chilling. The insulating layer retains heat next to your body, and is usually a (windproof) fleece jacket or sweater. The outer shell consists of a waterproof jacket that also protects against cold wind.

For the lower body, the layers generally consist of either shorts or loose-fitting trousers, thermal underwear ('long johns') and

waterproof overtrousers. When purchasing outdoor clothing, one of the most practical fabrics is merino wool. Though pricier than other materials, natural wool absorbs sweat, retains heat even when wet, and is soft and comfortable to wear. Even better, it doesn't store odors like other sports garments, so you can wear it for several days in a row without inflicting anti-social smells on your tent mates.

Waterproof Shells

Jackets should be made of a breathable, waterproof fabric, with a hood that is roomy enough to cover headwear, but that still allows peripheral vision. Other handy features include underarm zippers for easy ventilation and a large map pocket with a heavy-gauge zipper protected by a storm flap. Waterproof pants are best with slits for pocket access and long leg zips so that you can pull them on and off over your boots.

Footwear

Running shoes are OK for walks that are graded easy or moderate. However, you'll probably appreciate, if not need, the support and protection provided by hiking boots for more demanding walks. Non-slip soles (such as Vibram) provide the best grip.

Buy boots in warm conditions or go for a walk before trying them on, so that your feet can expand slightly, as they would on a hike. It's also a good idea to carry a pair of sandals to wear at night for getting in and out of tents easily or at rest stops. Sandals are also useful when fording waterways. Gaiters help to keep your feet dry in wet weather and on boggy ground; they can also deflect small stones or sand and maintain leg warmth. The best are made of strong fabric, with a robust zip protected by a flap, and secure easily around the foot. Walking socks should be free of ridged seams.

Backpack & Daypacks

For day walks, a day pack (30L to 40L) will usually suffice, but for multiday walks you will need a backpack of between 45L and 90L capacity. Even if the manufacturer claims your pack is waterproof, use heavy-duty liners.

Tent

A three-season tent will fulfill most walkers' requirements. The floor and the outer shell, or fly, should have taped or sealed seams and covered zips to stop leaks. The weight can be as low as 2.2lb (1kg) for a stripped-down, low-profile tent, and up to 6.6lb (3kg) for a roomy, luxury, four-season model. Dome- and tunnel-shaped tents handle windy conditions better than flat-sided tents.

★ Map & Compass

Always carry a good map of the area in which you are walking, and know how to read it. Buy a compass and learn how to use it. Make sure your compass is balanced for your destination zone. There are also 'universal' compasses on the market that can be used anywhere in the world.

Hiking Gear

A good walking stick or two lightweight ski poles will come in handy while hiking challenging uphill and downhill trails. Even if you intend to complete your hike before nightfall, bring along a flashlight just in case something happens and you can't make it back before sunset.

Emergency Supplies

Pack a first-aid kit and know what's in it. At a minimum, you'll want antiseptic wipes, bandages, gauze pads, medical tape and antibacterial ointment to treat cuts, scrapes and blisters. It should also include pain-relief medication (such as ibuprofen), insect-sting relief, antihistamine, tweezers and a pocket knife (or other multi-tool).

Don't forget to pack epinephrine if you're allergic to insect stings. Other useful items to have include an emergency Mylar blanket, a whistle and signal mirror for attracting attention and a fire starter (for an emergency survival fire).

Some hikers also travel with bear pepper spray. If you choose to bring it, make sure you know how to use it, and keep it handy (not stuffed in the bottom of your backpack) in case you need it.

Plan Your Trip
Great Lakes & Midwest's National Parks Overview

NAME	STATE	ENTRANCE FEE
Badlands National Park (p40)	South Dakota	7-day pass per vehicle $20
Cuyahoga Valley National Park (p46)	Ohio	Free
Gateway Arch National Park (p52)	Missouri	Free
Indiana Dunes National Park (p92)	Indiana	7-day pass per car/motorbike/person on foot or bicycle $25/20/15
Isle Royale National Park (p70)	Michigan	1-day pass per person $7
Theodore Roosevelt National Park (p76)	North Dakota	7-day pass per vehicle $30
Voyageurs National Park (p80)	Minnesota	Free
Wind Cave National Park (p82)	South Dakota	Free

Other NPS-Designated Sites & Areas

NAME	STATE	DESIGNATION
Apostle Islands (p72)	Wisconsin	National Lakeshore
Chimney Rock (p68)	Nebraska	National Historic Site
Effigy Mounds National Monument (p55)	Iowa	National Monument
Herbert Hoover National Historic Site (p55)	Iowa	National Historic Site

DESCRIPTION	GREAT FOR...
This otherworldly landscape, softened by its rainbow hues, is a spectacle of sheer walls and spikes stabbing the dry air.	
Along the winding Cuyahoga River, between Cleveland and Akron, this park is one of Ohio's nicest surprises.	
This is one of USA's smallest national parks, but its main attraction, the Gateway Arch, is the largest manmade monument in the US.	
The Dunes, which became the USA's 61st national park in 2019, stretch along 15 miles of Lake Michigan shoreline.	
This is certainly the place to go for peace and quiet; the 1200 moose creeping through the forest are all yours.	
Wildlife abounds in these surreal mounds of striated earth; sunset is particularly evocative as shadows dance across the lonely buttes.	
Voyageurs National Park is an outstanding mix of land and waterways formed from earthquakes, volcanoes and glaciers.	
Beneath the mixed-grass prairie and pine forest lies one of the world's longest, most complex cave systems.	

DESCRIPTION

Twenty-one rugged pieces of rock and turf floating in Lake Superior and freckling Wisconsin's northern tip; forested and windblown, trimmed with cliffs and caves, the national park gems have no facilities.

Eons-old bluff formations rise up from the horizon, their striking presence a dramatic sentinel connecting modern-day travelers with their pioneer forebears. Chimney Rock's fragile 120ft spire was an inspiring landmark for pioneers, and it was mentioned in hundreds of journals.

Hundreds of mysterious Native American burial mounds sit in the bluffs above the Mississippi River in this gorgeous corner of far northeast Iowa.

This complex preserves the house and some of the nearby structures from the time of Hoover's birth until age nine, when he was orphaned and left the area.

NAME	STATE	DESIGNATION
Homestead (p64)	Nebraska	National Historical Park
Jewel Cave (p88)	South Dakota	National Monument
Mississippi River (p75)	Minnesota	National River & Recreation Area
Missouri River (p74)	South Dakota & Nebraska	National Recreational River
Mount Rushmore (p86)	South Dakota	National Memorial
Niobrara National Scenic River (p74)	Nebraska	National Scenic River
Ozark National Scenic Riverways (p73)	Missouri	National Scenic Riverway
Pictured Rocks National Lakeshore (p72)	Michigan	National Lakeshore
Pony Express National Historical Trail (p66)	Nebraska	National Historical Trail
Scotts Bluff National Monument (p68)	Nebraska	National Monument
Silos & Smokestacks National Heritage Area (p54)	Iowa	National Heritage Area
Sleeping Bear Dunes National Lakeshore (p73)	Michigan	National Lakeshore
Trail of Tears National Historical Trail (p58)	Oklahoma	National Historical Trail
Washita Battlefield (p63)	Oklahoma	National Historical Trail

DESCRIPTION

The site of the very first homestead granted under the landmark Homestead Act of 1862, which opened much of the US to settlers who received land for free if they made it productive.

So named because calcite crystals line many of its walls. Currently 187 miles have been surveyed (3% of the estimated total), making it the third-longest known cave in the world.

The National Park Service operates a range of free ranger-guided activities here: in summer these include short hikes and bicycle rides; in winter, there are ice-fishing and snowshoeing jaunts.

Much of America's 19th-century sense of self was formed by events along the Missouri River, a 100-mile stretch of which is protected in the Missouri National Recreational River park.

George Washington, Thomas Jefferson, Abraham Lincoln and Theodore Roosevelt each iconically stare into the distance in 60ft-tall granite glory.

The winding canyons of the federally protected Niobrara National Scenic River in Nebraska draws scores of people through the summer for canoeing, kayaking and inner-tubing.

The Current and Jacks Fork Rivers boast 134 miles of splendid canoeing and inner-tubing (rental agencies abound). Weekends often get busy and boisterous.

Stretching along prime Lake Superior real estate, Michigan's Pictured Rocks National Lakeshore is a series of wild cliffs and caves, where blue and green minerals have streaked the red and yellow sandstone into a kaleidoscope of color.

The Pony Express (1860–61) was the FedEx of its day, using a fleet of young riders and swift horses to carry letters between Missouri and California in an astounding 10 days. Their route through Nebraska generally followed the Oregon Trail.

Scotts Bluff has been a beacon to travelers for centuries. Rising 800ft above the flat plains of western Nebraska, it was an important waypoint on the Oregon Trail in the mid-19th century. You can still see wagon ruts today.

Comprising 37 counties in northeast Iowa, this region includes more than 100 sites and attractions that honor the region's industrial past and storybook farm beauty.

Eye-popping lake views from atop colossal sand dunes? Water blue enough to be in the Caribbean? Miles of unspoiled beaches? Secluded islands with mystical trees? All here, along with lush forests, terrific day hikes and glass-clear waterways for paddling.

There's no soft-pedaling the Trail of Tears, the forced removal and march of five Indian tribes from the southeastern US to what was then called the Indian Territory in present-day eastern Oklahoma. The Trail of Tears National Historic Trail features important sites from the tragedy.

Marking the place where George Custer's troops launched a dawn attack on November 27, 1868 on the peaceful village of Chief Black Kettle

Road Trips

NAME	STATE	DISTANCE/DURATION
Black Hills Loop (p86)	South Dakota	265 miles / 2–3 days
Oklahoma's Tribal Trails (p58)	Oklahoma	453 miles / 4–5 days
On the Pioneer Trails (p64)	Nebraska	802 miles / 5–7 days

DESCRIPTION	ESSENTIAL PHOTO
Shaggy bison lumber across the plains. Giant monuments praise great men. Windswept prairies unfurl below towering mountains. This Black Hills tour embraces the region's heritage in all its messy glory.	Find a new angle on the four mugs at Mt Rushmore.
This trip takes in some of the sites (and others) on the Oklahoma stretch of the Trail of Tears National Historic Trail, which features important sites from the tragic forced removal and march of five Indian tribes from the southeastern US to what was then called the Indian Territory in present-day eastern Oklahoma..	Dawn at Washita Battlefield National Historic Site.
Follow in the wagon tracks of thousands of pioneers who crossed Nebraska on iconic treks like the Oregon Trail. Visit windswept settlements of those who stayed behind.	The postcard-worthy buttes of Scotts Bluff.

Plan Your Trip
Best Hiking

Top:left: Maah Daah Hey Trail, Theodore Roosevelt National Park (p76); Top right: Fall colors, Indiana Dunes State Park
Bottom: Notch Trail, Badlands National Park (p40)

Nothing encapsulates the spirit of the national parks like hiking. You'll find countless trails in the Great Lakes and the Midwest that offer access to craggy overlooks, picturesque waterfalls and wildlife-filled forests.

Maah Daah Hey Trail, Theodore Roosevelt

Make the ultimate trek through the North Dakota Badlands on this 144-mile trek that takes you past windswept prairies, over rocky peaks, along meandering rivers and through sun-backed valleys.

Notch Trail, Badlands

A short but spectacular trail that takes you through a canyon, up a wooden ladder and along a clifftop for sweeping views over the Badlands. Visit close to sunrise or sunset to beat the crowds.

Stoll Memorial Trail, Isle Royale

Walk through pine forest and out along rugged shorelines to a serene point overlooking Lake Superior. If you're still hungering for more, you can link up with other trails that stretch across this 46-mile-long island.

Three-Dune Loop, Indiana Dunes

Get in your workout for the week on a hike up the three highest dunes in the national park. You'll ascend 552 vertical feet and enjoy lofty views over Lake Michigan.

Plan Your Trip
Best Wildlife Watching

Top left: Upland sandpiper bird, Custer State Park (p88); Top right: Resting wolf, Voyageurs National Park (p80)
Bottom: Bison, Sage Creek Rim Road, Badlands National Park (p40)

From tiny prairie dogs to 2000lb bison, this biologically diverse region harbors an astonishing variety of wildlife. Wherever you roam, try to time your visits for dawn or dusk to maximize your chances of animal encounters.

Sage Creek Rim Road, Badlands

Take it slow as you drive this dirt road through the less-visited section of the Badlands. Bison spotting is common, and you can also check out some massive prairie dog 'towns'.

Rainy Lake, Voyageurs

Foxes, moose, black bears and wolves all live in the forests abutting Rainy Lake. There are countless opportunities to see and hear wildlife, whether canoeing the waterways, hiking the trails or camping by the shore.

Apostle Islands National Lakeshore

Situated along a key flyway on the Great Lakes, this rugged shoreline is a prime stop for migrating birds in spring and fall. Even in the summer you can see unique species.

Custer State Park

Home to over 200 bird species and the largest bison herds in North America, this South Dakota reserve is a must for wildlife lovers.

Plan Your Trip
Best Family Experiences

Above: Sleeping Bear Dunes (p73); Top right: Cuyahoga Valley Scenic Railroad (p47);
Bottom right: Crazy Horse Memorial (p90)

Pulling kids (and adults) off their screens and into a national park can be a transformative experience. It's also a great chance for the whole family to enjoy some time together outdoors, whether checking out waterfalls or looking for stars in pollution-free night skies.

Cave Tour, Wind Cave

Many miles of subterranean passageways lie hidden in western South Dakota. Various cave tours showcase the magic of this national park. For an old-fashioned experience, visit less-developed sections on the Candlelight Tour.

Dune Climbing, Sleeping Bear Dunes

It's good fun to slog your way up to the top of a towering sand dune or just play in nature's biggest sand box. The best part of the adventure is racing back down the dunes.

Train Ride, Cuyahoga Valley

Take a trip aboard the vintage Cuyahoga Valley Scenic Railroad as it chugs through its namesake park. With key stops along the way, you can combine a ride with a hike or bike ride.

Crazy Horse Memorial

By day visit a Native American museum and the studio of Korczak Ziolkowski, sculptor of the large-scale monument. Then at night return for a well-done light show on the mountain that taps into the history and myths of the great Sioux nation.

Plan Your Trip
Best Adventures

Above: Kekekabic Lake, Boundary Waters (p73); Top right: Houseboat, Voyageurs National Park (p80); Bottom right: Night camping, Isle Royale (p70)

LEFT: WILDNERDPIX/SHUTTERSTOCK ©; TOP RIGHT: REBECCA SCHWARTZ/SHUTTERSTOCK ©; BOTTOM RIGHT: MATIPON/SHUTTERSTOCK ©

Home to the biggest freshwater system on the planet, not to mention thousands of islands and endless miles of pristine shoreline, the Great Lakes region is unrivaled when it comes to adventures on and along the water.

Paddling, Boundary Waters Canoe Wilderness Area

You could spend a few days or a few lifetimes exploring this island-dotted reserve in northern Minnesota. There's no better place on earth for a canoeing and camping adventure.

Inner Tubing, Niobrara National Scenic River

Enjoy a leisurely day floating down a section of the Niobrara River. You'll pass waterfalls, river bluffs and woodlands along the way. Those seeking a bigger adventure can make it a multi-day kayak or canoe trip.

Houseboating, Voyageurs

If you don't want to paddle, you can hire a well-equipped houseboat for your trip to Voyageurs. This is a great way to find your own slice of paradise in this magnificent park.

Lakeside Camping, Isle Royale

You'll find dozens of beautiful waterfront sites on Isle Royale. Many overlook Lake Superior, while some are set on inland lakes reachable only by canoe.

Badlands National Park, South Dakota

GREAT LAKES & MIDWEST USA

NAUGHTYNUT/SHUTTERSTOCK ©

Badlands Loop Road

Badlands National Park

Named mako sica *(badland) by Native Americans, this national park's other-worldly landscape is a spectacle of sheer walls and spikes stabbing the dry air, softened by its fantastic rainbow hues. Gazing upon its striking formations from the corrugated walls surrounding the park is like seeing an ocean boiled dry.*

Great For...

State
South Dakota

Entrance Fee
7-day pass per car/person on foot, motorcycle or bicycle $20/10

Area
379 sq miles

The north unit of the park is easily viewed on a drive, though there are a number of short hiking trails that can get you right out into this earthen wonderland. The less-accessible south units are in the Pine Ridge Indian Reservation and see few visitors. Bisecting the two is Hwy 44.

Badlands Loop Road
Stunning Highway 240 is easily reached from I-90 (exits 110 and 131) and you can drive it in an hour if you're in a hurry (and not stuck behind an RV). It is the main thoroughfare in the park's north unit, with lookouts, vistas and animal sightings aplenty.

Sage Creek Rim Road
The portion of the Badlands west of Hwy 240 along this gravel road is much less visited than the sights of the Badlands Loop Rd. There are scenic overlooks and stops at prairie-dog towns; this is where most backcountry hikers and campers go

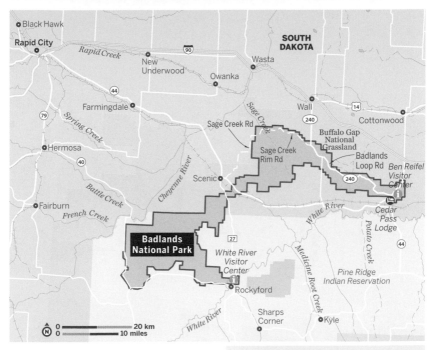

to escape the crowds. As there is almost no water or shade here, don't strike out into the wilderness unprepared.

Buffalo Gap National Grassland

The Badlands, along with the surrounding Buffalo Gap National Grassland, protects the country's largest prairie grasslands, several species of Great Plains mammal (including bison and black-footed ferret), prairie falcons and lots of snakes. Rangers can map out back-road routes that will let you do looping tours of Badlands National Park and the grasslands without ever touching I-90.

Sleeping & Eating

The park has two campgrounds and a seasonal lodge. Hotels can be found on I-90 in Kadoka and Wall. There are also campgrounds and inns near the southern entrance at Interior. There are restaurants of varying quality in Wall and Interior.

Essential Information

The park is 60 miles east of Rapid City, exiting I-90 at Wall. There's no public transportation to (or within) the park.

Ben Reifel Visitor Center (☑605-433-5361; www.nps.gov/badl; Hwy 240; ☺7am-7pm Jun-Aug, 8am-5pm Apr, May, Sep & Oct, 8am-4pm Nov-Mar) The main visitor center. Don't miss the on-site paleontology lab.

National Grasslands Visitor Center (☑605-279-2125; www.fs.fed.us/grasslands; 708 Main St, Wall; ☺8am-4:30pm Mon-Fri) Has good displays on the wealth of life in this complex ecosystem.

White River Visitor Center (Hwy 27; ☺9am-4pm Jun-Aug) Small information outlet in the little-visited south unit.

Stay at a cozy cabin inside the park at **Cedar Pass Lodge** (☑605-433-5460; www. cedarpasslodge.com; Hwy 240; d $176; ☺mid-Apr–mid-Oct; ❄@). There is a restaurant and shops. ∎

Big Horn Sheep

EASTCOTT MOMATIUK/GETTY IMAGES ©

Wildlife of the Great Plains

Great Plains national parks protect large swaths of forest and grassland where bison, elk and wild horses roam. There are also hundreds of bird species, and innumerable prairie dogs in sprawling subterranean towns.

Mule Deer

Somewhere along your journey you're likely to encounter mule deer, named for their large mule-like ears, as they browse on leaves and twigs from shrubs. Look for them around dusk, grazing in herds.

Bison

Bison nearly met extinction because of hunting and human encroachment; by the 20th century, only a few hundred remained. Overcoming near extinction, new herds arose from these last survivors, so that one of America's noblest animals can again be admired in its gruff majesty – among other places, in Badlands, Theodore Roosevelt and Wind Cave National Parks.

Pronghorn Antelope

Curious-looking deer-like animals with two single black horns instead of antlers, pronghorns belong to a unique antelope family. They are only found in the American West, but they are more famous for being able to run up to 60mph for long stretches; they're the second-fastest land animal in the world.

Prairie Dogs

The prairie dog is neither a prairie-dweller nor a dog: related to the squirrel, it lives in sprawling burrows known as prairie dog 'towns.'

Elk

Seeing a herd of North American elk, or *wapiti* (a Native American name meaning 'white rump,' a description of the animal's rear), grazing in their natural setting is unforgettable. Full-grown males may reach 1100lb and carry 5ft racks of antlers.

KENNETH SPONSLER/SHUTTERSTOCK ©

Ohio & Erie Canal

Cuyahoga Valley National Park

Ohio's only national park has a mystical beauty, especially on a cold morning when the mists thread the woods and all you hear is the sound of a great blue heron flapping over its hunting grounds. Its Native American name is 'crooked river' or possibly 'place of the jawbone.'

Great For...

State
Ohio

Entrance Fee
Free

Area
51 sq miles

Brandywine Falls

This pretty spill of ice-cold water sits nestled in a wooden idyll, and can be accessed via a 1.5-mile round-trip hike that features some light-elevation (160ft) gain. A small bridge and a boardwalk lookout make this a visitor favorite.

Hiking & Cycling

The park's main trail follows the old **Ohio & Erie Canal**. Boats pulled by mules once ran adjacent to this trail, now an ideal thoroughfare for hikers and cyclists. Information about the canal and towpath is available at the **Canal Exploration Center** (☏216-524-3537; www.nps.gov/cuva; 7104 Canal Rd; ⊙10am-4pm Jun-Aug, limited hours rest of year).

The most photographed place is probably **The Ledges** overlook. There's a moderately difficult loop trail nearby, a little over 2 miles in length.

The 5.3-mile **Old Carriage Trail**, past forested ledges, streams and a 500-foot

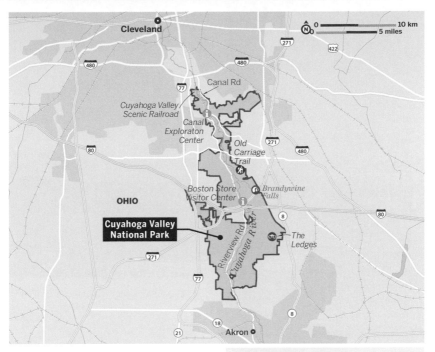

ravine, is one of the longer loop trails, but it's not particularly difficult.

Scenic Railroad

An old-school iron carriage chugs along the pleasant **Cuyahoga Valley Scenic Railroad** (CVSR; ✆800-468-4070; www.cvsr.com; adult $16-29, child $11-24) course from Akron to Independence, OH, through the heart of the park. The most expensive tickets score seating in the glass-topped 'dome.' A full round-trip takes around 3½ hours. You can take a bicycle on board ($5; April to October).

Camping & Lodging

There are five primitive campsites within the park, available for booking from late May through October ($25; www.reserveamerica.com). Bring water. The park is close enough to Cleveland or Akron for a day trip, and there are some more posh lodging options in Peninsula.

Essential Information

The park is easily accessible by car from Cleveland (20 miles) or Akron (18 miles), and lies just off of I-77.

Boston Store Visitor Center (✆330-657-2752; www.nps.gov/cuva/planyourvisit/boston-store; 1550 Boston Mills Rd; ⏰9:30am-5pm Sep-May, 8am-6pm Jun-Aug) A historic warehouse-cum-information depot, this center serves as the main visitor hub for the park. You can get updated information on any trail closures here, as well as detailed maps. If there is a lecture, ranger walk or visiting expert or artist at the park, all of the above will be based out of this building.

The Inn at Brandywine Falls (✆330-467-1812; www.innatbrandywinefalls.com; 8230 Brandywine Rd, Northfield; d $149-229, ste $239-349; ❄️🛜), an 1848 Greek Revival country home, has six individually differentiated rooms and delicious breakfasts. ■

The Great Lakes

The Great Lakes are huge, like inland seas, offering beaches, dunes, resort towns and lighthouse-dotted scenery. Four of the five (Lakes Erie, Huron, Superior and Michigan) are in the Midwest. While Michigan is entirely within the US, the other four lay across the US–Canada border.

Lake Ontario

Lake Ontario is the smallest and most easterly of the interconnected Great Lakes.

Lake Michigan

In addition to **Indiana Dunes National Park** (☎219-926-7561; www.nps.gov/indu; 1100 N Mineral Springs Rd, Porter; ☉6am-11pm) **FREE**, miles of Lake Michigan's unspoiled beaches, secluded islands, lush forests and glass-clear water are protected in the Sleeping Bear Dunes National Lakeshore (p73).

Lake Huron

Lake Huron (together with Lake Superior) is the USA's most unexpected dive spot, with thousands of shipwrecks lying strewn on the sandy bottoms – just don't expect to see any angelfish!

Lake Erie

In 1812's Battle of Lake Erie, Admiral Perry met the enemy English fleet near South Bass Island. **Perry's Victory & International Peace Memorial** (www.nps.gov/pevi; 93 Delaware Ave, South Bass Island; adult/child $10/free; ☺10am-6pm mid-May–mid-Oct), a 352ft Doric column, is now a singular attraction. Take the elevator to the observation deck for views of Lake Erie, the islands and, on a good day, Canada.

JOHN MCCORMICK/SHUTTERSTOCK ©

Lake Superior

Lake Superior boasts Isle Royale National Park (p70); Pictured Rocks National Lakeshore (above and top right, p72), with its series of wild cliffs and caves, where blue and green minerals have streaked the red and yellow sandstone into a kaleidoscope of color; and Apostle Islands National Lakeshore (top right, p72), which encompasses 21 rugged pieces of forested and windblown rock and turf, trimmed with cliffs and caves.

ARCHITECT: EERO SAARINEN, IMAGE: FLIPHOTO/SHUTTERSTOCK. ©

Gateway Arch National Park

Officially dedicated as a national park in 2018, the park's footprint is small, fitting snugly into downtown St Louis along the Mississippi River. But its main attraction, the Gateway Arch, dominates the city's skyline and pays tribute to the Lewis and Clark expedition and westward expansion of the US.

Great For...

State
Missouri

Entrance Fee
Free

Area
0.14 sq miles

Gateway Arch

As a symbol for St Louis, the Gateway Arch has soared above any expectations its backers could have had in 1965 when it opened. The **Arch** (☏877-982-1410; www.gatewayarch.com; tram ride adult/child $13/10; ⊘8am-10pm Jun-Aug, 9am-6pm Sep-May, last tram 1hr before closing), designed by Eero Saarinen, serves as both a monument to the country's old western frontier and as an unmistakable icon for the city. At 630ft tall, it's the largest manmade monument in the US (more than twice as tall as the Statue of Liberty). A short tram ride to the top lets you take in the view, but tram cars can be a tight squeeze as they clank their way skyward.

Back on the ground, you can walk right up and touch the Arch's base, and kids will swear they can see the structure swaying in the wind as they look up (it is designed to do so, but only actually does in severe weather).

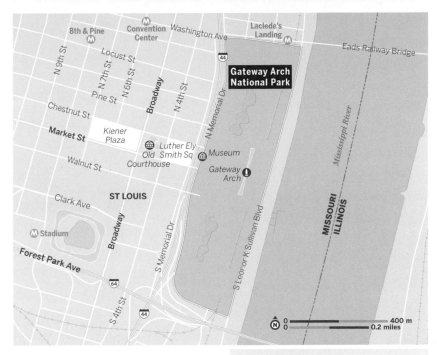

Old Courthouse

Free to enter, this **historic structure** (11 North 4th St; ⊘8am-4:30pm) was the site of two trials in the Dred Scott case, now considered among the very worst US Supreme Court decisions. Scott, an enslaved man who attempted to sue for his freedom, was denied standing to bring the suit. Now a museum, the courthouse's galleries deal with the ignominious history of slavery and the fight for emancipation.

Historical Museum

After receiving a facelift along with the rest of the park and reopening in summer 2018, this museum not only offers more high-tech interactive exhibits but an updated historical view of westward expansion, with displays acknowledging that the West was either 'won' or stolen, depending on your perspective. Visitors can also learn about the innovative engineering behind the Arch monument. ∎

Essential Information

If you're in downtown St Louis, just look up and walk towards the giant silver arch. Can't miss it.

A greenway now seamlessly covers the highway that used to divide the arch grounds from the courthouse and rest of downtown.

Those further afield can take I-64, I-44 or I-55 into the city. There's no dedicated parking directly on-site, so look for a spot in the nearby Laclede's Landing bar district or in one of the garages around Busch Stadium (just not on a gameday). Public transportation options include the Metrolink light rail, which stops at Laclede's Landing, or city buses 99 and 40.

The park grounds are open daily from 5am to 11pm.

Silos & Smokestacks National Heritage Area

Comprising 37 counties in northeast Iowa, this National Park Service–designated region includes more than 100 sites and attractions that honor the region's industrial past and storybook farm beauty.

Amana Colonies

These rustic villages were established as German religious communes between 1855 and 1861 by Inspirationists who, until the Great Depression, lived a utopian life with no wages paid and all assets communally owned. Unlike the Amish and Mennonite religions, Inspirationists embrace modern technology (and tourism).

National Mississippi River Museum & Aquarium

Learn about life (of all sorts) along the length of the Mississippi at this impressive museum, part of a vast riverfront development. Exhibits span steamboating, aquatic life and indigenous Mississippi River dwellers. Interactive exhibits include touch ponds where you can feel a jellyfish, among other critters.

Effigy Mounds National Monument

Hundreds of mysterious Native American burial mounds sit in the bluffs above the Mississippi River in this gorgeous corner of far northeast Iowa (p102). Listen to songbirds as you hike the lush trails.

Herbert Hoover National Historic Site

Herbert Hoover, the president of the United States from 1929 to 1933, will forever be remembered for the Great Depression, the economic cataclysm that wiped out the livelihoods of millions. However, he lived a long life (1874–1964) and devoted much of it to public service. This complex preserves the house and some of the nearby structures from the time of his birth until age nine, when he was orphaned and left the area. The museum places his life into context.

AMEL DIZDAREVIC/ALAMY ©

John Deere Tractor & Engine Museum

Close to downtown Waterloo, this museum celebrates all things John Deere and is a fantasy come true for tractor-heads. It's part of the Deere research center.

KEVIN E. SCHMIDT/QUAD-CITY TIMES/ZUMA WIRE/ALAMY ©

Mines of Spain Recreation Area

This vast expanse of Mississippi River Bluffland just south of Dubuque offers 12 miles of hiking trails with scenic overlooks, picnic facilities and even a wildlife observation blind. Head to the EB Lyons Interpretive Center to learn about the landscape and plan your visit.

State Historical Museum of Iowa

At the foot of the capitol, this modern museum features first-person accounts from people who lived through different historical eras and events. Yes, there's a lot of farm implements but there's also 'Hollywood in the Heartland' with details on how films like Field of Dreams and The Bridges of Madison County were made in the state.

National Czech & Slovak Museum & Library

Interactive exhibits and oral histories tell the stories of the Czech and Slovak immigrants who came to the US and built Cedar Rapids. Special exhibitions throughout the year dive deep into their cultural experience.

CLASSIC ROAD TRIPS

Road Trip: Oklahoma's Tribal Trails

There's no soft-pedaling the **Trail of Tears**, the forced removal and march of five Indian tribes from the southeastern US to what was then called the Indian Territory in present-day eastern Oklahoma. The tales of death, deception and duplicity are sobering. The National Park Service administers the Trail of Tears National Historic Trail (www.nps.gov/trte), which features important sites from the tragedy. This trip takes in some of those sites (and others) across Oklahoma. In addition you can learn about the vital role of Native Americans in the state today.

Distance 453 miles/729km

Duration 4–5 day

Best Time to Go

Enjoy this trip April to October, when the weather can be lovely.

Essential Photo

Dawn at Washita Battlefield National Historic Site.

Best for History

The unmissable Cherokee Heritage Center with its moving displays in Tahlequah.

❶ Tahlequah

Subtle, forested hills interspersed with lakes and iconic red dirt cover Oklahoma's northeast corner, aka Green Country (www.greencountryok.com), which includes Tahlequah, the Cherokee capital since 1839.

Of the tragedies visited on Indian tribes, perhaps none is more tragic than the relocation of the Cherokees. The history and horror behind the forced march is movingly traced at the six-gallery Cherokee Heritage Center outside of town. Interactive displays describe key events, including court battles and stockade imprisonment, that preceded the forced removal, then focus on the army-commanded marches between 1838 and 1839. Disease, starvation and the cold killed scores on the 800-mile journey. Outside, at the Ancient Village, visitors can learn what life was like in a Cherokee community before the arrival of Europeans. The one-hour guided tour includes pottery-making and blowgun demonstrations.

The Drive » The Cherokee Heritage Center is on the south side of Tahlequah. From here it is a short drive (1 mile) south on South Keeler Dr to your next stop.

❷ Hunter's Home

A large estate from the mid-19th century, this historic house belies some of the images of the Cherokees as downtrodden. George Murrell, who was of European descent, was married to Minerva Ross, a member of a prominent Cherokee family (her uncle was principal chief of the tribe from 1828 to 1866). He moved with his family at the time of the forced removals and built this estate, which offers a look at the more genteel aspects of life in the early days of the Indian Territory.

The Drive » The third stop on the tour is an easy 18 miles southwest along US 62. Enjoy the gently rolling countryside and iconic red Oklahoma earth.

❸ Fort Gibson

Built as a frontier fort in 1824, Fort Gibson came to play an integral – and notorious

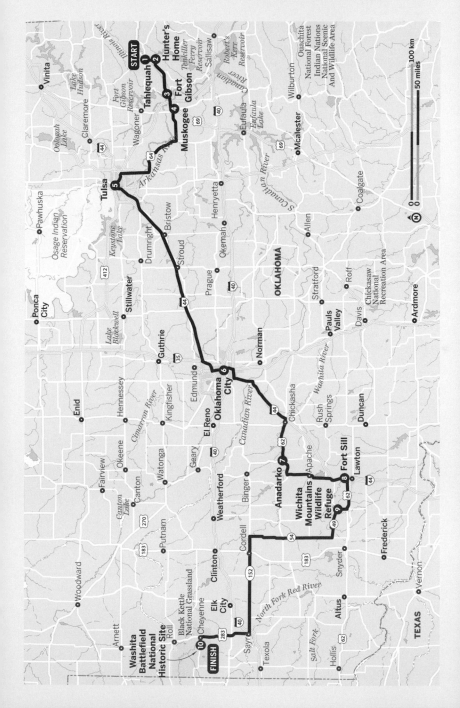

– role in the Trail of Tears. It was home to the removal commission in the 1830s and is where surviving Creek and Seminole people were brought after the forced march. From here they were dispatched around the Indian Territory. You can get a good sense of military life 180 years ago at the restored grounds and buildings. Fort Gibson is a National Historic Landmark managed by the Oklahoma Historical Society. Washington Irving wrote his landmark *A Tour of the Prairies* in 1835 based on trips he took with Fort Gibson troops in 1832 and 1833 looking for local bands of Native Americans.

The Drive »Continue southwest on US 62 to Muskogee, 9 miles away.

❹ Muskogee

The namesake of Merle Haggard's 1969 hit *Okie from Muskogee*, this place is a bit different from the rest of Oklahoma. It is deep in the Arkansas River Valley and there are hints of humid air from the Gulf of Mexico. Here you can learn more about the relocated tribes at the small but engaging Five Civilized Tribes Museum. The museum is located in an 1875 former Indian Agency office that was used as a meeting place for the leaders of the five tribes. The museum dedicates one wall to each tribe; displays cover an eclectic array of topics from Choctaw code talkers in WWI to variations in lacrosse sticks. The gift shop sells pottery, painting and jewelry made by members of the five tribes.

The Drive »Skip the tolls and monotony of the Muskogee Turnpike and opt instead for US 64, which wanders through classic small towns such as Haskell that give a timeless sense of rural Oklahoma. The 60-mile drive to Tulsa will take about 90 minutes.

❺ Tulsa

Self-billed as the 'Oil Capital of the World,' Tulsa is home to scores of energy companies that make their living drilling for oil, selling it or supplying those who do. The wealth this provides once helped create Tulsa's richly detailed art-deco downtown

and has funded some excellent museums that give the state's Native American heritage its due. The superb Gilcrease Museum has a great story: it sits on the manicured estate of Thomas Gilcrease, a part–Native American who grew up on Creek tribal lands. He was ater eligible for a tribal allotment that contained a little surprise: oil.

Over his life, Gilcrease built up one of the world's great collections of art and artifacts relating to the American West cultures. The museum is northwest of downtown, off Hwy 64. South of town is another oil magnate's property, a converted Italianate villa also ringed by fabulous foliage. It houses some fine Native American works at the Philbrook Museum of Art.

The Drive »Link Oklahoma's two largest cities via the quick route of I-44, otherwise known as the Turner Turnpike. In return for the tolls you'll minimize your time between the big-name attractions as you zip along slightly more than 100 miles.

❻ Oklahoma City

At the impressive Oklahoma History Center you can explore the heritage of the 39 tribes headquartered in the state. Artifacts include an 1890 cradleboard, a Kiowa pictorial calendar and an original letter from Thomas Jefferson that Lewis and Clark gave to the Otoe tribe. In it, Jefferson invites the tribe to the nation's capital. Be sure to look up before you leave – there's a Pawnee star chart on the ceiling. You can experience the frontier in a manner more familiar to anyone who has seen an old Western movie at the National Cowboy & Western Heritage Museum.

The Drive »A 40-mile drive southwest on I-44 (the Bailey Turnpike toll road) leads to Chickasha at exit 83. Head 20 miles west on US 62 through Native American lands to Anadarko.

❼ Anadarko

Eight tribal lands are located in this area, and students from many more tribes are enrolled in Anadarko schools. The town regularly hosts powwows and Native

Top: Cherokee National Museum, Cherokee Heritage Center (p58);
Bottom: The Indian Union Agency building houses the Five Civilized Tribes Museum

(8) Five Civilised Tribes

Two of eastern Oklahoma's earliest known tribes, the Osage and the Quapaw, ceded millions of acres to the US government in the 1820s. The US then gave the land to five east-coast tribes: the Cherokee, Chickasaw, Choctaw, Creek and Seminole. Because these five tribes had implemented formal governmental and agricultural practices in their communities, they were collectively called the Five Civilized Tribes. The Five Civilized Tribes were forced to move to the Oklahoma area, known then as the Indian Territory, after settlers in the southern states decided they wanted the tribes' fertile farmlands for themselves. Between 1830 and 1850, the five tribes were forcibly relocated; their routes are collectively known as the Trail of Tears. How many people died in this forced march is unknown, however records suggest deaths were in the tens of thousands. Often overlooked are the thousands of African Americans who were held as slaves by the Native Americans. Scores died during the removals. As for their new homes in the Indian Territory, the US government said it would belong to the five tribes as long as the stars shine and rivers flow. The reality? More like 70 years. In the mid-1800s the country was quickly expanding west, and white settlers wanted the land. Through legislative maneuvering, certain Indian-owned lands were deemed 'unassigned,' opening them up for settlement. The Oklahoma Land Rush began on April 22, 1889, when 50,000 would-be settlers made a mad dash for their own 160-acre allotment.

American events. To mix a little shopping with your learning, visit Oklahoma Indian Arts & Crafts Co-Op, which sells museum-quality crafts, including jewelry, dolls and beadwork items (barrettes, purses and moccasins). About 85% of the store's customers are Native American. You can also visit the Southern Plains Indian Museum, which houses a small but diverse collection of Plains Indian clothing, weaponry and musical instruments. Just east is the National Hall of Fame for Famous American Indians. A short outdoor walk leads past the bronze busts of well-known Native Americans including Pocahontas, Geronimo and Sitting Bull. The visitor center has a good selection of books on Oklahoma Indians.

The Drive » US 62 continues to figure prominently in this tour as you drive 35 miles south to Fort Sill. The historic portion is just west of US 62 on the edge of this very active military base.

❽ Fort Sill

Oklahoma isn't just home to eastern tribes. Numerous western and Plains tribes, including the Apache, Comanche, Kiowa and Wichita, were also forced here as the US expanded west. The US Army built Fort Sill in 1869 in Kiowa and Comanche territory to prevent raids into settlements in Texas and Kansas. By the 1880s and 1890s its role had changed, and the fort was serving as a protective sanctuary for many tribes. The Fort Sill National Historic Landmark & Museum, which fills several original stone buildings, explores the history of the fort. Another highlight is the 1872 Post Guardhouse, the center of law enforcement for the Indian Territory. Step inside to see where Apache leader Geronimo was detained on three separate occasions. Geronimo's grave is on fort grounds a few miles from the guardhouse. Fort Sill remains an active army base. You'll need to register at the Visitors Control Center before passing through the gates to view the historic sites.

The Drive » Leave booming artillery in your wake as you roll west on Hwy 62 to state Hwy 115 north. Black-eyed susans, scrubby trees and barbed-wire fences line the two-lane byway as it unfurls from tiny Cache toward the hill-dappled Wichita Mountains Wildlife Refuge.

❾ Wichita Mountains Wildlife Refuge

Southwest Oklahoma opens into expansive prairie fields all the way to Texas. Beautiful mountains provide texture. The 59,020-acre Wichita Mountains Wildlife Refuge protects bison, elk, longhorn cattle and a super-active prairie dog town. Wildlife is abundant; observant drivers might even see a spindly, palm-sized tarantula tiptoeing across the road. At the visitor center, informative displays highlight the refuge's flora and fauna. A massive glass window yields inspiring views of prairie grasslands. For a short but scenic hike, try the creek-hugging Kite Trail to the waterfalls and rocks at the Forty Foot Hole. It starts at the Lost Lake Picnic Area.

The Drive » After 15 miles on Hwy 49, turn north on Hwy 54, which runs through tribal lands. Look for schools, tiny towns and small farms on the 38.5 miles. At Hwy 152, just north of Cloud Chief village, turn west for 44 miles to US 283. Go north for 24 miles to Cheyenne and follow the signs to the Washita site.

❿ Washita Battlefield National Historic Site

Marking the place where George Custer's troops launched a dawn attack on November 27, 1868 on the peaceful village of Chief Black Kettle is Washita Battlefield National Historic Site. It was a slaughter of men, women, children and domestic animals, an act some would say led to karmic revenge on Custer eight years later.

Among those who died was the peace-promoting chief, Black Kettle. Even today, you may encounter current members of the US military studying what exactly transpired here that cold, pre-winter morning. Self-guiding trails at the site traverse the site of the killings, which is remarkably unchanged.

A visitor center 0.7 miles away contains a good museum. Seasonal tours and talks are very worthwhile. A small garden shows how traditional plants were grown for medicine, spiritual rituals and food.

IRINAK/SHUTTERSTOCK ©

American bison, Wichita Mountains Wildlife Refuge

CLASSIC ROAD TRIPS

Road Trip: On the Pioneer Trails

Balmy days driving through lush green valleys and barren buttes; nights hanging outside a small-town ice-cream stand recalling the day's adventures to the background sound of crickets. These are just some of the charms of exploring the back roads of Nebraska, which, like the ubiquitous state plant, corn, when left on the fire, pops with attractions. Eschew I-80 and be a modern-day pioneer. This road trip takes in a selection of NPS designated sites and monuments, among other points of interest.

Distance: 802 miles/1290km
Duration: 5–7 Days

Best Time to Go
May to September when everything is open and the wildflowers are in bloom.

Essential Photo
The postcard-worthy buttes of Scotts Bluff.

Best for Exploring
Off-the-beaten-path explorations of a land many blithely whiz through.

❶ Omaha

Omaha's location on the Missouri River and proximity to the Platte made it an important stop on the Oregon, California and Mormon Trails. Many heading west paused here before plunging into Nebraska and you should do the same. Learn tales from these pioneer trails at the beautiful Durham Museum, housed in the once-bustling Union Station.

The Drive » Scoot along US 6 with its old drive-ins still peddling soft-serve cones and other pleasures for the 57 miles to Lincoln.

❷ Lincoln
Home to the historic Haymarket District and the huge downtown campus of the University of Nebraska, the capital city is a good place to get the big picture of the state's story. You can almost hear the wagon wheels creaking and the sound of sod busting at the Nebraska History Museum.

The Drive » Drive 35 miles south of Lincoln on Hwy 77 to Beatrice.

❸ Beatrice - Homestead National Monument of America
The Homestead National Monument just west of Beatrice is on the site of the very first homestead granted under the landmark Homestead Act of 1862, which opened much of the US to settlers who received land for free if they made it productive. The pioneering Freeman family is buried here and you can see their reconstructed log house and hike the site. The heritage center is a striking building with good displays.

The Drive » An even 100 miles west on US 136 takes you through near ghost towns, where the solitary gas stations serve as town centers and quaint brick downtowns slowly crumble. Head north at Red Cloud and drive for 68 miles on US 281.

❹ Grand Island
For a wide-ranging introduction to pioneer life, spend a few hours at the 200-acre

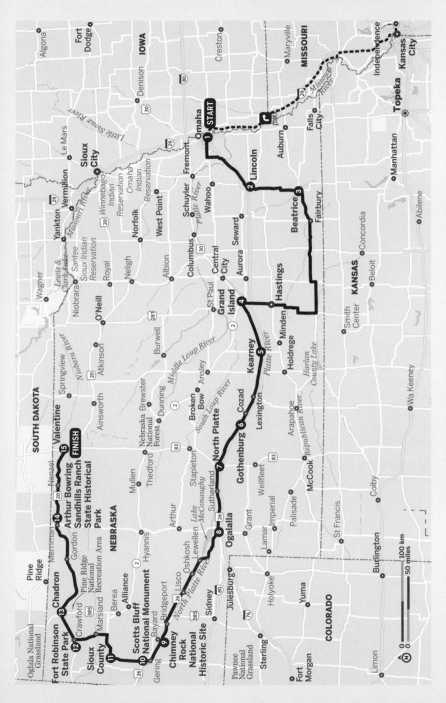

ⓘ Avoid I-80

I-80 zips across Nebraska for 455 miles. But while it speeds travelers on their way, it does the state no favors. Here are some fine alternatives: take US 6 out of Omaha to Lincoln, US 34 on to Grand Island and then historic US 30 – the original Lincoln Highway – all the way to Wyoming.

Stuhr Museum of the Prairie Pioneer in Grand Island. In summer, period reenactors go about their business in an 1890s railroad town, answering questions about their jobs and home life. Also on view is an 1860s log-cabin settlement, a one-room schoolhouse and a Pawnee earth lodge.

On the 2nd floor of the museum's Stuhr Building, a covered wagon overflows with furniture and clothes – an inspiring symbol of the pioneers' can-do optimism. A few steps away, a display of black-and-white photos of a primitive sod house and a prairie funeral depict the darker, harsher realities lurking behind the romance of the pioneer dream. Interesting fact? In 1880, 20% of Nebraska's population was foreign born, with most settlers emigrating from Germany, Sweden and Ireland.

The Drive » The leaves of cottonwoods shimmer in the sunlight on this lonely yet lush 42 miles of US 30.

❺ Kearney

A shimmering brown arch sweeps across four lanes of I-80 like an imposing medieval drawbridge. This horizon-breaking distraction – it depicts a setting Nebraska sun – is the Great Platte River Road Archway Monument. A little bit hokey, a little bit history, it's a relentlessly cheery ode to the West that puts a high-tech, glossy spin on the pioneer journey, sweeping in everything from stampeding buffalo to the gold-seeking forty-niners. Afterwards drive 10 minutes southeast to Fort Kearny State Historical Park, which preserves the fort that protected travelers on the Oregon and California Trails. Kearney's compact, cute and walkable downtown, near US 30 and

the busy Union Pacific main line, has good cafes and craft breweries.

The Drive » Count the grain silos and see if they outnumber the passing trains along the next 60 miles of US 30.

❻ Gothenburg: Pony Express

The Pony Express (1860–61) was the FedEx of its day, using a fleet of young riders and swift horses to carry letters between Missouri and California in an astounding 10 days. Each horseman rode full-bore for almost six hours – changing horses every 10 miles – before passing the mail to the next rider. Their route through Nebraska generally followed the Oregon Trail. In Gothenburg, step inside what some researchers think is an original Pony Express Station, one of just a few still in existence. The engaging array of artifacts includes a mochila, the rider's mail-holding saddlebag. Afterwards, wander a few of the streets downtown lined with beautiful old Victorian houses.

The Drive » A never-ending procession of UP trains zip along the world's busiest freight line for the next 36 miles of US 30.

❼ North Platte

North Platte, a rail-fan mecca, is home to the Buffalo Bill Ranch State Historical Park, 2 miles north of US 30. Once the home of Bill Cody – an iconic figure of the American West and the father of rodeo and the famed Wild West show – it has a fun museum that reflects his colorful life. Enjoy sweeping views of UP's Bailey Yard, the world's largest railroad classification yard, from the Golden Spike Tower, an eight-story observation tower with indoor and outdoor decks.

The Drive » Set the cruise control on 'chill' as you drive a straight line 52 miles due west on US 30.

❽ Ogalalla

Set your clocks to mountain time just west of Sutherland. Ogalalla was once known as the 'Gomorrah of the Cattle Trail.' It now

Top: University of Nebraska, Lincoln; **Bottom:** Buffalo Bill Ranch State Historical Park

Go West!

An estimated 400,000 people trekked west across America between 1840 and 1860, lured by tales of gold, promises of religious freedom and visions of fertile farmland. They were also inspired by the expansionist credo of President James Polk and the rallying cry of New York editor John O'Sullivan, who urged Americans in 1845 to 'overspread the continent allotted by Providence for the free development of our yearly multiplying millions.'

These starry-eyed pioneers became the foot soldiers of Manifest Destiny, eager to pursue their own dreams while furthering America's expansionist goals. The movement's success depended on the safe, reliable passage of these foot soldiers through the Great Plains and beyond. The California, Oregon and Mormon pioneer trails served this purpose well, successfully channeling the travelers and their prairie schooners on defined routes across the country.

has all the salacious charm of a motel's nightstand bible. The Oregon and California Trails turn north near here, following the Platte River toward Wyoming and the wild blue yonder.

The Drive » Cornfields give way to untamed prairie grasses and desolate bluffs on two-lane US 26, known as Nebraska's Western Trails Historic & Scenic Byway. Look right soon after leaving Ogallala to glimpse sparkling Lake McConaughy through the low hills. Otherwise, cattle herds, passing trains with coal from Wyoming and tumbleweed towns are the biggest distractions for the next 101 miles.

⑨ Chimney Rock National Historic Site

Heading west, centuries-old bluff formations rise up from the horizon, their striking presence a visual link connecting modern-day travelers (and Oregon Trail gamers) with their pioneer forebears. One of these links is Chimney Rock, located inside the Chimney Rock National Historic Site. It's visible 12 miles after Bridgeport off Hwy 92. Chimney Rock's fragile 120ft spire was an inspiring landmark for pioneers, and it was mentioned in hundreds of journals. It also marked the end of the first leg of the journey and the beginning of the tough – but final – push to the coast.

The Drive » Stay on Hwy 92 for 21 miles west after Chimney Rock. As you enter Gering, just south of the city of Scottsbluff, continue straight onto M St, which leads to Old Oregon Trail Rd. It follows the actual route of the trail and leads straight to Scotts Bluff National Monument after just 3 miles.

⑩ Scotts Bluff National Monument

Spend a few minutes in the visitor center of this picturesque monument run by the National Park Service – there's a nice collection of Western art in the William Henry Jackson Gallery – then hit the trail. You can hike the 1.6-mile (one way) Saddle Rock Trail or drive the same distance up to the South Overlook for bird's-eye views of Mitchell Pass. Before you leave, spend a few moments hiking the trail through Mitchell Pass itself. The covered wagons on display here look unnervingly frail as you peer through the bluff-flanked gateway, a narrow channel that spills onto the Rocky Mountain–bumping plains. For pioneers, reaching this pass was a significant milestone; it marked the completion of 600 miles of Great Plains trekking.

The Drive » From Scottsbluff, leave the Great Platte River Rd and head north to a historic military fort and a lonely trading post, important bastions that paved the way for long-term settlers. Along the way, revel in Nebraska's prairie, which is aptly described as a 'sea of grass.' This analogy proves true on the 52-mile drive north on Hwy 71.

⑪ Sioux County

Prairie grasses bend and bob as strong winds sweep over low-rolling hills, punctuated by the occasional wooden windmill or lonely cell-phone tower as you drive through Sioux County, named for the Plains tribe that hunted and traveled throughout Nebraska. Enjoy the drive: this is roll-down-your-window-and-breathe-in-America country.

The Drive » Like bristles on the visage of a trail-weary pioneer, trees begin appearing amid the rolling grasslands as you head north for 27 miles on Hwy 2.

⑫ Fort Robinson State Park

Sioux warrior Crazy Horse was fatally stabbed on the grounds of Fort Robinson, now Fort Robinson State Park, on September 5, 1877, at the age of 35. The fort – in operation between 1874 and 1948 – was the area's most important military post during the Indian Wars. In summer, visitors descend on the 22,000-acre park for stagecoach rides, steak cookouts, trout fishing and hiking. There are two museums on the grounds – the Fort Robinson Museum and the Trailside Museum – as well as the reconstructed Guardhouse where Crazy Horse spent his final hours.

The Drive » If you prefer your historic digs in an urban setting, drive 20 miles east to Chadron.

⑬ Chadron

Chadron's Museum of the Fur Trade is a well-curated tribute to the mountain men and trappers who paved the way for the pioneers. It holds a fascinating array of artifacts: from 1820s mountain-man leggings and hand-forged animal traps to blankets, pelts and liquor bottles. Kit Carson's shotgun is displayed beside the world's largest collection of Native American trade guns. Out back, there's a reproduction of the Bordeaux Trading Post; it was in operation here from 1837 to 1876. The harsh reality of life on the plains is evident the moment you step inside the unnervingly cramped building. Though it's not the original struc-

ture, the reproduction is so precisely done that it's listed on the National Register of Historic Places.

The Drive » Continue east to the Sandhills for 77 miles on US 20, known as the Bridges to Buttes Byway. The little towns along here are just hanging on amid the buttes, canyons and rolling hills of the often-dramatic landscape.

⑭ Arthur Bowring Sandhills Ranch State Historical Park

The hardscrabble lives of Nebraskan ranchers is faithfully recalled at this preserved 1920s ranch near the South Dakota border. Owned by the Bowring clan, it includes an early sod house that makes it clear that any farmhouse was a major step up. Still, you'll find comforts here as Eva Bowring, who lived here for much of her long life, collected drool-worthy crystal, china and antique furniture.

The Drive » Keep the camera ready for moody shots of lonely windmills amid the sandy bluffs on the 60 miles east on US 20 to Valentine.

⑮ Valentine

What better way to literally immerse yourself in a timeless Nebraska from before the pioneer days than floating down a scenic river – especially on a steamy summer day. Valentine sits on the edge of the Sandhills and is a great base for canoeing, kayaking and inner-tubing the winding canyons of the federally protected Niobrara National Scenic River (www.nps.gov/niob). The river crosses the Fort Niobrara National Wildlife Refuge. Driving tours take you past bison, elk and more. Floating down the river draws scores of people through the summer. Sheer limestone bluffs, lush forests and spring-fed waterfalls along the banks shatter any 'flat Nebraska' stereotypes. Most float tours are based in Valentine (www.visitvalentine.com).

STEVE LAGRECA/SHUTTERSTOCK ©

Rock Harbor Lighthouse

Isle Royale National Park

Totally free of vehicles and roads, Isle Royale National Park in Lake Superior is the place to go for peace and quiet. It gets fewer visitors in a year than Yellowstone National Park gets in a day, which means the 1600 moose creeping through the forest are all yours.

Great For...

State
Michigan

Entrance Fee
1-day pass per person $7

Area
210 sq miles

The island is laced with 165 miles of hiking trails that connect dozens of campgrounds along Superior and inland lakes. You must be totally prepared for this wilderness adventure, with a tent, camping stove, sleeping bags, food and water filter. The park is open from mid-April through October, then it closes due to extreme weather.

Sleeping & Eating

Isle Royale offers two options: snooze with lake views at **Rock Harbor Lodge** (☎906-337-4993; www.rockharborlodge.com; r/cottage from $260/504; ☺late May-early Sep) or hike to the rustic campgrounds with outhouses that dot the island. There's no extra fee for camping – it's covered in the $7 per day park entrance fee.

The lodge has two eateries: a dining room serving American fare and a more casual cafe. The Dockside Storeat Rock

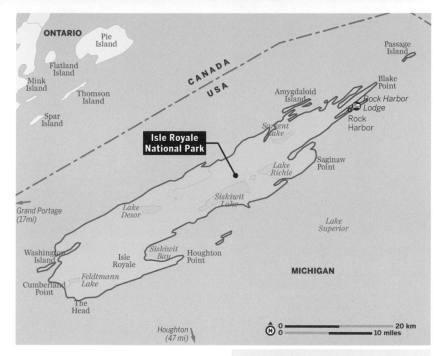

Harbor stocks a small array of groceries and there's another small store in Windigo. Prices are steep.

Getting There & Around

Reserve transportation well in advance. From the dock outside the park headquarters in Houghton, the **Ranger III** (☺late May-early Sep) departs at 9am on Tuesday and Friday for the six-hour boat trip (one way adult/child $70/35) to Rock Harbor, at the east end of the island.

Isle Royale Seaplanes (☎906-483-4991; www.isleroyaleseaplanes.com; 21125 Royce Rd, Hancock) is quicker, flying from the Portage Canal Seaplane Base in Hancock to Rock Harbor or to Windigo (the island's west end) in 35 minutes (round-trip $320).

Or head 50 miles up the Keweenaw Peninsula to Copper Harbor and jump on the **Isle Royale Queen IV** (☎906-289-4437;

Essential Information

Isle Royale Park Headquarters (☎906-482-0984; www.nps.gov/isro; 800 E Lakeshore Dr, Houghton; ☺8am-6pm Mon-Fri, from 10am Sat Jun–mid-Sep, 8am-4pm Mon-Fri mid-Sep–May) The park headquarters in Houghton provides information on entrance fees, ferries, camping etc.

www.isleroyale.com; 14 Waterfront Landing, Copper Harbor), an 8am 3½-hour crossing (round-trip adult/child $136/100), running daily from late July through August. Bringing a kayak or canoe on the ferries costs an additional $50 round-trip.

You can also access Isle Royale from Grand Portage, MN on the **Voyageur II** and **Seahunter III** (☎218-600-0765; www.isleroyaleboats.com; 402 Upper Road, Grand Portage). ∎

National Lakeshores & Rivers

Pictured Rocks

Stretching along prime Lake Superior real estate, Michigan's Pictured Rocks National Lakeshore is a series of wild cliffs and caves, where blue and green minerals have streaked the red and yellow sandstone into a kaleidoscope of color.

Apostle Islands

The National Park Service's Apostle Islands, 21 rugged pieces of rock and turf floating in Lake Superior and freckling Wisconsin's northern tip, are a state highlight. Forested and windblown, trimmed with cliffs and caves, the national park gems have no facilities.

STEVEN SCHREMP/SHUTTERSTOCK ©

Ozark National Scenic Riverways

North of US 60, Missouri, the Ozark National Scenic Riverways – the Current and Jacks Fork Rivers – boast 134 miles of splendid canoeing and inner-tubing (rental agencies abound). Weekends often get busy and boisterous.

PAPER AND LENS CO/SHUTTERSTOCK ©

Sleeping Bear Dunes

Eye-popping lake views from atop colossal sand dunes? Water blue enough to be in the Caribbean? Miles of unspoiled beaches? Secluded islands with mystical trees? All here at Sleeping Bear Dunes, Michigan (p110), along with lush forests, terrific day hikes and glass-clear waterways for paddling.

WILDNERDPIX/SHUTTERSTOCK ©

Boundary Waters

Although not part of the National Park Service (managed instead by the US Forest Service), the Boundary Waters Canoe Wilderness Area (p108), legendarily remote and pristine, is one of the world's premier paddling regions. More than 1000 lakes and streams speckle the piney, 1.1-million-acre expanse. Nature lovers make the pilgrimage for the miles of canoe routes, rich wildlife and sweeping solitude.

MAREKULIASZ/SHUTTERSTOCK ©

Niobrara National Scenic River

The winding canyons of the federally protected Niobrara National Scenic River in Nebraska draw scores of people through the summer for canoeing, kayaking and inner-tubing.

JOSEPH SOHM/SHUTTERSTOCK ©

Missouri River

Much of America's 19th-century sense of self was formed by events along the Missouri River, a 100-mile stretch of which is protected in the Missouri National Recreational River park. In 1804–05, Lewis and Clark followed the Missouri River during the first stages of their legendary journey west, meeting Native Americans – some friendly, others hostile – and discovering vast expanses of land, untouched for eons and teeming with wildlife.

Porcupine Mountains Wilderness State Park

A Keweenaw Heritage Site (an official partner of NPS's Keweenaw National Historical Park), Porcupine Mountains Wilderness State Park, Michigan, is known for its waterfalls, 20 miles of undeveloped Lake Superior shoreline, black bears lumbering about, and the view of the park's stunning Lake of the Clouds.

Mississippi River

The National Park Service operates a range of free ranger-guided activities in Minnesota's Mississippi National River & Recreation Area. In summer these include short hikes and bicycle rides. In winter, there are ice-fishing and snowshoeing jaunts.

ZAK ZEINERT/SHUTTERSTOCK ©

Theodore Roosevelt National Park

Wildlife abounds in these surreal mounds of striated earth, from mule deer to wild horses, bison, bighorn sheep and elk. Sunrise is the best time for animal encounters, while sunset is particularly evocative as shadows dance across the lonely buttes, painting them in an array of earth tones before they fade to black.

Great For...

State
North Dakota

Entrance Fee
7-day pass per car/motorcycle/person on foot or bicycle $30/25/15

Area
110 sq miles

The park is divided into North and South Units, 70 miles apart. South Unit, near Medora, houses the main visitor center and is closer to the interstate highway (I-94). The more remote North Unit is 15 miles south of Watford City.

Hiking

In the South Unit, the 0.4-mile **Wind Canyon Trail** leads to a dramatic viewpoint over the Little Missouri River. The slightly more strenuous 0.6-mile **Coal Vein Trail** traces the history of a coal vein that caught fire and burned for 26 years in the mid-20th century.

In the less visited North Unit, the 1.5-mile **Buckhorn Trail** leads to Prairie Dog Town, a favorite spot for observing these animated little critters. The challenging but spectacular 18-mile **Achenbach Trail** crosses the Little Missouri River twice and dips through American bison habitat: you'll see where bison roll on their backs for a dust bath.

Essential Information

South Unit Visitor Center (www.nps.gov/
thro; off I-94 exits 24 & 27, Medora; ⊘8am-
5pm Jun-Sep, to 4:30pm Oct-May) Bookstore,
museum and information on ranger-led
activities.

Teddy Roosevelt's Cabin

Future president Theodore Roosevelt
retreated from New York to this remote
spot after losing both his wife and mother
in a matter of hours. The 25-year-old future
president spent the winter of 1883–84
here, and it's said that his time in the
Dakota badlands inspired him to become
an avid conservationist – he set aside 230
million acres of federal land while in office.

Behind the South Unit Visitor Center, the
cabin is faithfully reconstructed using its
original Ponderosa pine logs. It houses a
few artifacts belonging to Roosevelt, including a writing desk and a traveling trunk.

Horseback Riding

History buffs and adventurous spirits will
find it hard to resist seeing these landscapes as Roosevelt himself did, on horseback. The 144-mile **Maah Daah Hey Trail**,
which links the park's North and South
Units, passes through a dauntingly rugged,
scenic stretch of badlands.

Sleeping & Eating

The resort town of Medora makes a great
base with comfortable lodgings across all
budgets. The park itself has two campgrounds, including the more popular
Cottonwood Campground in the South
Unit. Wild camping is permitted in the backcountry for up to 14 consecutive nights; get
a free permit at either visitor center. Pets,
bicycles and motorized vehicles are strictly
prohibited in the backcountry. Hazards to
watch out for include ticks, poison ivy, scor-
pions, snakes and fast-moving bison.

Medora is the only place to eat near
the South Unit Visitor Center, while less-
attractive Watford City is closer to the
less-visited North Unit. ■

Top Left: Wild Horses **Bottom Left:** Black Tailed Deer

WIRESTOCK CREATURES/SHUTTERSTOCK ©

Above: Wind Canyon, Little Missouri River

GEORGE BURBA/SHUTTERSTOCK ©

Voyageurs National Park

It's all about water up in Voyageurs National Park, most of which is accessible only by hiking or motorboat. In the 17th century, French-Canadian fur traders began exploring the Great Lakes and northern rivers by canoe. The park covers part of their customary waterway, which became the border between the USA and Canada.

Great For...

State
Minnesota

Entrance Fee
Free

Area
341 sq miles

Boat Tours & Houseboats

The park operates **boat tours** (📞218-286-5258; www.recreation.gov; 2½hr tours adult/child $30/15; ⊘2pm Wed & Fri-Mon mid-Jun–early Sep, 2pm Mon & Wed mid-Sep) to see eagles, an 1890s gold-mining camp and more. It's best to reserve in advance. The park also offers free, 1½-hour jaunts in mighty voyageur canoes from late June to mid-August.

Novice boaters are welcome at family-run **Ebel's Voyageur Houseboats** (📞218-374-3 571; www.ebels.com; 10326 Ash River Trail; per day from $335; ⊘early May–early Oct). The pricier houseboats have air-conditioning, DVD players and hot tubs.

Winter Sports

When the boats get put away for the winter, the snowmobiles come out. Voyageurs is a hot spot for the sport, with 110 miles of staked and groomed trails slicing through the pines. Rainy Lake Visitor Center

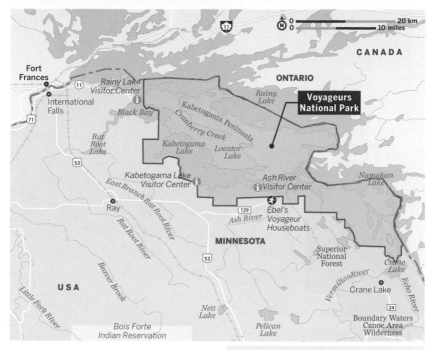

provides maps and advice. It also lends out snowshoes and cross-country skis for local trails, including a couple that depart outside the center.

To the south, an ice road for cars spans the boat launches of the Ash River and Kabetogama Lake Visitor Centers. A fun sledding hill also plunges near the Kabetogama center.

Sleeping & Eating

Far-flung resorts and camping are the choices, aside from sleeping on your own houseboat. Restaurants are few and usually connected to lodges. The communities of Kabetogama, Crane Lake, Ash River and International Falls hold the majority of places to eat.

Destination Voyageurs National Park (www.dvnpmn.com) has lodging and activity details for the park's gateway communities. ∎

Essential Information

Hwy 53 is the main highway to the region. It's about a five-hour drive from the Twin Cities (or a three-hour drive from Duluth) to Crane Lake, Ash River or Lake Kabetogama. International Falls, near the park's northwest edge, holds the closest airport.

Rainy Lake Visitor Center (☏218-286-5258; www.nps.gov/voya; Hwy 11; ☺9am-5pm daily Jun-Aug, 9am-5pm Sat-Wed Sep, 10am-4pm Thu-Sun Oct-May) Eleven miles east of International Falls on Hwy 11, this is the main park office. Ranger-guided walks and boat tours are available here in summer, and equipment rentals in winter.

Ash River (☏218-374-3221; Mead Wood Rd; ☺9am-5pm late May–late Sep) and **Kabetogama Lake** (☏218-875-2111; off Hwy 53; ☺9am-5pm late May–late Sep) Seasonal visitor centers, both of which offer ranger-led programs.

ZACK FRANK/SHUTTERSTOCK ©

Wind Cave National Park

Above ground, Wind Cave National Park protects forests and grasslands where bison, elk and prairie dogs roam. But the central draw is below ground: Wind Cave, containing 148 miles of mapped passages, is one of the world's longest underground realms. Strong gusts at the entrance give the cave its name.

Great For...

State
South Dakota

Entrance Fee
Free

Area
44 sq miles

Cave Tours

Several **tours** ($10 to $30) plunge you into the scene. The easiest is the hour-long **Garden of Eden Tour**, a 0.33-mile walk. The most strenuous is the four-hour **Wild Cave Tour**, where you crawl and climb through further-flung passages. The moderate **Natural Entrance Tour** is the most popular, while the romantic **Candlelight Tour** dips into less-developed sections of the cave, lit only by – that's right – candles.

Hiking

Back at the surface, hikers reap big rewards on 30 miles of unspoiled trails that ramble through rolling prairie and pine forest. **Rankin Ridge** is an easy walk where you amble up a one-mile path to an old fire tower, the park's highest point. The **Cold Brook Canyon Trail** is a moderate 2.8-mile hike that takes in meadows, a prairie dog town and falcon-laden cliffs. The **Centennial Trail** is a bit more difficult, meandering

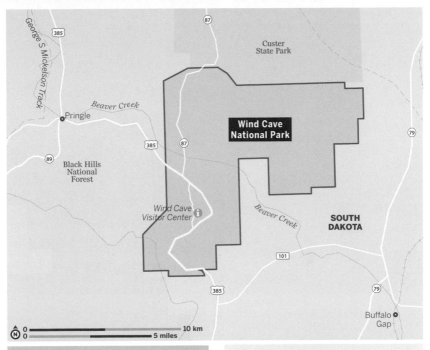

Rock Formations

The cave's foremost feature is its 'boxwork' calcite formations, which look like honeycomb and date back 60 to 100 million years. Wind Cave is one of the few places where you can see boxwork, along with strange formations such as popcorn, moon milk, frostwork and gypsum flowers.

Essential Information

The nearest airport is 60 miles away in Rapid City. There's no public transport.

Wind Cave Visitor Center (☎605-745-4600; www.nps.gov/wica; off US 385; ⊙8am-4:30pm daily, expanded hours Jun-Aug) Has exhibits, maps and books and is the place to go for tour details and bookings, and camping permits.

six miles one way through patches of prairie and along Beaver Creek.

Wildlife Spotting

Wildlife watchers get an eyeful driving the park's rustic roads. Keep an eye out for large herds of bison, elk and pronghorn antelope that wander the plains munching fresh grass. Prairie dog towns see lots of action, and not just from the cute main characters, but also from sneaky coyotes and slithering black-footed ferrets. The town at the intersection of Hwys 385 and 87 provides a good peek at the scene.

Sleeping

The park (www.nps.gov/wica) has one campground with flush toilets (no showers or electricity). The 62 campsites (per night $18) are available first-come, first-served. Backcountry camping is allowed in certain areas; get a free permit from the visitor center. ■

Top Left: Boxwork formations Bottom Left: Black-tail Prairie Dog

CLASSIC ROAD TRIPS

Road Trip: Black Hills Loop

In the early 1800s, 60 million buffalo roamed the plains. Rampant overhunting decimated their ranks and by 1889 fewer than 1000 remained. Today, their numbers have climbed to 500,000; several Black Hills parks manage healthy herds. On this tour, which takes in Wind Cave National Park and other NPS designated sites, among other things, you'll see the iconic buffalo and other legendary sights, including the Badlands, Mt Rushmore, the Crazy Horse Memorial, sprawling parks and the town made famous for having no law: Deadwood.

Distance: 265 miles/426km
Duration: 2–3 Days

Best Time to Go

May to September, when all sights are open.

Essential Photo

Find a new angle on the four mugs at Mt Rushmore.

Best for Outdoors

Where buffalo roam is just the start of critter-filled days amid beautiful scenery.

❶ Rapid City

A worthy capital to the region, 'Rapid' has a lively and walkable downtown. Well-preserved brick buildings, filled with shops and places to dine, make it a good urban base and hub for your looping tour. Get a walking-tour brochure of Rapid's historic buildings and public art from the visitor center. Check out the watery fun on Main St Square. While strolling, don't miss the Statues of Presidents on downtown street corners. From a shifty-eyed Nixon in repose to a triumphant Harry Truman, lifelike statues dot corners throughout the center. Learn about how dramatic natural underground events over the eons have produced some spectacular rocks. See these plus dinosaur bones and some stellar fossils at the Museum of Geology at the South Dakota School of Mines & Technology.

The Drive » Choose from the commercial charms on Hwys 16 and 16A on the 21-mile drive to Keystone.

❷ Keystone

One indisputable fact about the Black Hills? It will always, always, always take longer than you think to reach a key attraction. Trust us. Slow-moving Winnebagos, serpentine byways and kitschy roadside distractions will deaden your pace. And the distractions start early on Hwy 16 where family-friendly and delightfully hokey tourist attractions vie for dollars on the way to Mt Rushmore, including the animal-happy Bear Country USA and Reptile Gardens. Kitsch reigns supreme in Keystone, a gaudy town bursting with rah-rah patriotism, Old West spirit and too many fudgeries. The fuss is directly attributable to its proximity to Mt Rushmore, 3 miles west.

The Drive » It's a mere 3-mile jaunt uphill to Mt Rushmore. Keep yours eyes peeled for the first glimpse of a president.

❸ Mt Rushmore National Memorial

Glimpses of Washington's nose from the roads leading to this hugely popular monument never cease to surprise and are but harbingers of the full impact of this mountainside sculpture once you're up close (and past the less impressive parking area and entrance walk). George Washington, Thomas Jefferson, Abraham Lincoln and Theodore Roosevelt each iconically stare into the distance in 60ft-tall granite glory. Hugely popular, you can easily escape the crowds and fully appreciate Mt Rushmore while marveling at the artistry of sculptor Gutzon Borglum and the immense labor of the workers who created the memorial between 1927 and 1941.

The Presidential Trail loop passes right below the monument for some fine nostril views and gives you access to the worthwhile Sculptor's Studio. Start clockwise and you're right under Washington's nose in under five minutes. The nature trail to the right as you face the entrance connects the viewing and parking areas, passing through a pine forest and avoiding the crowds and commercialism.

The official Park Service information center has an excellent bookstore with proceeds going to the park. Avoid the schlocky Xanterra gift shop and the disappointing Carvers Cafe, which looked much better in the scene where Cary Grant gets plugged in *North by Northwest*. The main museum is far from comprehensive but the fascinating Sculptor's Studio conveys the drama of how the monument came to be.

The Drive » Backtrack slightly from Mt Rushmore and head southwest for 16 miles of thrills on the Iron Mountain Rd.

❹ Peter Norbeck Scenic Byway

Driving the 66-mile Peter Norbeck Scenic Byway is like flirting with a brand-new crush: always exhilarating, occasionally challenging and sometimes you get a few butterflies. Named for the South Dakota senator who pushed for its creation in 1919, the oval-shaped byway is broken into four

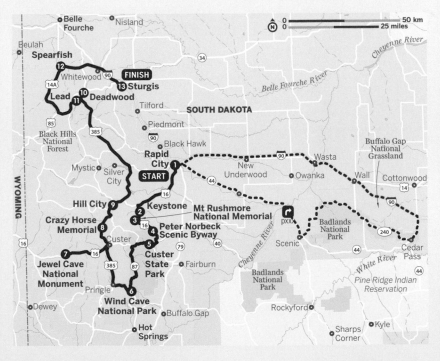

roads linking the most memorable destinations in the Black Hills (drivers of large RVs should call Custer State Park for tunnel measurements).

Iron Mountain Rd (Hwy 16A) is the real star, beloved for its pigtailing loops, Mt Rushmore–framing tunnels and one gorgeous glide through sun-dappled pines. It's a 16-mile roller coaster of wooden bridges, virtual loop-the-loops, narrow tunnels and stunning vistas. Expect lots of drivers going even slower than you are. The 14-mile Needles Hwy (Hwy 87) swoops below granite spires, careens past rocky overlooks and slings though a supernarrow tunnel.

The Drive » Once past the Iron Mountain Rd, other Peter Norbeck Scenic Byway options aside, it is only 3 miles along Hwy 16 west to the Custer State Park visitor center.

❺ Custer State Park

The only reason 111-sq-mile Custer State Park isn't a national park is that the state grabbed it first. It boasts one of the largest free-roaming bison herds in the world (about 1500), the famous 'begging burros' (donkeys seeking handouts) and more than 200 bird species. Other wildlife include elk, pronghorns, mountain goats, bighorn sheep, coyotes, prairie dogs, mountain lions and bobcats. Meandering over awesome stone bridges and across sublime alpine meadows, the 18-mile Wildlife Loop Road allows plenty of spotting.

The Custer State Park Visitor Center, situated on the eastern side of the park, contains good exhibits and offers guided nature walks. The nearby Black Hills Playhouse hosts summer theater.

Hiking through the pine-covered hills and prairie grassland is a great way to see wildlife and rock formations. Trails through Sylvan Lake Shore, Sunday Gulch, Cathedral Spires and French Creek Natural Area are all highly recommended.

The park is named for the notorious George A Custer, who led a scientific expedition into the Black Hills in 1874. The expedition's discovery of gold drew so many new settlers that an 1868 treaty granting

the Sioux a 60-million-acre reservation in the area was eventually broken. Crazy Horse and the Lakotas retaliated, killing Custer and 265 of his men at Montana's Battle of the Little Big Horn in 1876.

The Drive » Near the western edge of Custer State Park, head due south on Hwy 87 for 19 miles from US 16. It's a beautiful ride through a long swath of wilderness and park.

❻ Wind Cave National Park

This park, protecting 44 sq miles of grassland and forest, sits just south of Custer State Park. The central feature is, of course, the cave, which contains 147 miles of mapped passages. The cave's foremost feature is its 'boxwork' calcite formations (95% of all that are known exist here), which look like honeycomb and date back 60 to 100 million years. The strong gusts of wind that are felt at the entrance, but not inside, give the cave its name.

The COVID-19 pandemic put a damper on tours, but luckily, not all of the park's treasures are underground. Wind Cave's above-ground acres abound with bison and prairie dogs.

The Drive » Scenic drives continue as you go from one big hole in the ground to another. Jewel Cave is 38 miles northwest on US 385 and US 16.

❼ Jewel Cave National Monument

Another of the Black Hills' many fascinating caves is Jewel Cave, 13 miles west of Custer on US 16, so named because calcite crystals line many of its walls. Currently 187 miles have been surveyed (3% of the estimated total), making it the third-longest known cave in the world. You can check at the visitor center if tours (fees apply) are happening (they were paused due to the Covid-19 pandemic). If not, try one of the trails that depart right outside of the center.

The Drive » Retrace your route for 13 miles until US 385 joins US 16 and then go north for 5 miles.

CHERI ALGUIRE/SHUTTERSTOCK ©

ALEX GIMBAL/SHUTTERSTOCK ©

Top: Boxwork geological rock formation, Wind Cave; **Bottom**: Custer State Park

⑧ Crazy Horse Memorial

The world's largest monument, the Crazy Horse Memorial is a 563ft-tall work-in-progress. When finished it will depict the Sioux leader astride his horse, pointing to the horizon saying, 'My lands are where my dead lie buried.'

Never photographed or persuaded to sign a meaningless treaty, Crazy Horse was chosen for a monument that Lakota Sioux elders hoped would balance the presidential focus of Mt Rushmore. In 1948 a Boston-born sculptor, the indefatigable Korczak Ziolkowski, started blasting granite. His family have continued the work since his death in 1982. (It should be noted that many Native Americans oppose the monument as desecration of sacred land.) No one is predicting when the sculpture will be complete (the face was dedicated in 1998). A rather thrilling laser-light show tells the tales of the monument on summer evenings.

The visitor center complex includes a Native American museum, a cultural center, cafes and Ziolkowski's studio.

The Drive » It's a short 10-mile drive north on US 16/385 to the refreshments of Hill City.

⑨ Hill City

One of the most appealing towns up in the hills, Hill City (www.hillcitysd.com) is less frenzied than places such as Keystone. Its main drag has cafes and galleries.

The 1880 Train is a classic steam train running through rugged country to and from Keystone. An interesting train museum is next door.

The Drive » Lakes, rivers, meadows and a few low-key tourist traps enliven the 42 miles on US 385 to Deadwood through the heart of the Black Hills.

⑩ Deadwood

Fans of the HBO TV series may recall that Deadwood was the epitome of lawlessness in the 1870s. Today things have changed, although the 80 gambling halls, big and small, would no doubt put a sly grin on the faces of the hard characters who founded the town.

Deadwood's atmospheric streets are lined with gold-rush-era buildings lavishly restored with gambling dollars. Its storied past is easy to find at its museums and cemeteries. There's eternal devotion to Wild Bill Hickok, who was shot in the back of the head here in 1876 while gambling.

Actors reenact famous shootouts on Main St during summer, including the 1877 saloon fight between Tom Smith and David Lunt (who lived for 67 days relatively unbothered by the bullet in his head before finally dropping dead).

The Drive >> Lead is just 4 miles uphill from Deadwood, through land scarred by generations hunting for gold.

⑪ Lead

Lead (pronounced 'leed') has slowly gentrifying charm but still bears plenty of scars from the mining era. Gape at the 1250ft-deep open-pit mine from the Sanford Lab Homestake Visitor Center to see what open-pit mining can do to a mountain. Nearby are the same mine's shafts, which plunge more than 1.5 miles below the surface and are now being used for physics research.

The Drive » Climb out of steep canyons for 11 miles on US 14A until you plunge back down into Spearfish Canyon.

⑫ Spearfish

Spearfish Canyon Scenic Byway (www.spearfishcanyon.com/scenicbyway) is a waterfall-lined, curvaceous 20-mile road that cleaves from the heart of the hills into Spearfish. There's a sight worth stopping for around every bend; pause for longer than a minute and you'll hear beavers hard at work.

The Drive » It's a quick 22 miles east on I-90 to Sturgis. That solitary headlight in the rearview mirror is a hog hoping to blow past. From Sturgis back to Rapid City is only 36 miles.

Crazy Horse Memorial

⑬ Sturgis

Neon-lit tattoo parlors, Christian iconography and billboards for ribald biker bars featuring dolled-up models are just some of the cacophony of images of this loud and proud biker town. Shop for leather on Main St, don your American flag bandana and sidle up to the saloon bar to give a toast to the stars and stripes. Things get even louder for the annual Sturgis Motorcycle Rally, when around 700,000 riders, fans and curious onlookers take over the town.

Dunes Ridge Trail

Indiana Dunes National Park

The Dunes, which became the USA's 61st national park in 2019, stretch along 15 miles of Lake Michigan shoreline. Swimming is allowed anywhere along the shore. A short walk away from the beaches, several hiking paths crisscross the dunes and woodlands, where blue herons flock (though there's no actual rookery) and native wildflowers bloom.

Oddly, all this natural bounty lies smack-dab next to smoke-belching factories, which you'll also see at various vantage points, but it's not without its superlatives: it boasts 1100 native species of plants and dunes, formed after melted glaciers, which top out at 192ft. If you're wondering what to do in the Hoosier state, this is its most visited site, attracting some 3.5 million visitors per year.

Activities

Hiking, birding, fishing, biking, paddling and beachcombing are some of the most popular activities at the Indiana Dunes.

Don't miss the 3 Dune Challenge, a 1.5-mile, 552ft vertical climb to the park's three highest dunes: Mt Jackson (176ft), Mt Holden (184ft) and Mt Tom (192ft).

Great For...

State
Indiana

Entrance Fee
7-day pass per car/motorbike/person on foot or bicycle $25/20/15

Area
Over 22,000 sq miles

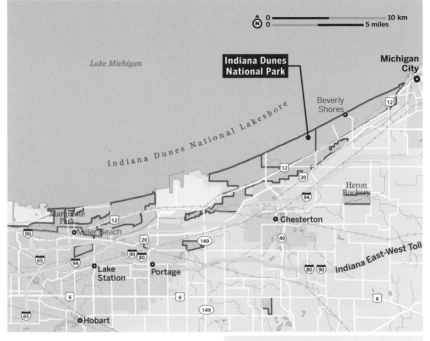

Trail 7

The 1.1-mile Trail 7 near the state park Nature Center provides direct dune-and-beach access.

Indiana Dunes State Park

Indiana Dunes State Park is a 2100-acre, shoreside pocket within the national park; it's located at the end of Hwy 49, near Chesterton. It has more amenities than the rest of the lakeshore, but also more regulation and crowds (plus a vehicle entry fee of Indiana/out-of state license plates $7/12). Wintertime brings out the cross-country skiers; summertime brings out the hikers. Seven trails zigzag over the landscape; No 8 up Mt Tom rewards with Chicago skyline views.

Essential Information

Getting There & Away

The Indiana Toll Rd (I-80/90), I-94, Hwy 12, Hwy 20 and Hwy 49 all skirt the lakeshore. Look for large brown signs on the roads that point the way in to the Dunes.

The **South Shore Line** commuter train (www.mysouthshoreline.com) also services the area on its Chicago–South Bend route. The stops at Dune Park and Beverly Shores put you about a 1½-mile walk from the beaches.

Visitor Center The best place to start a visit to the Dunes is at the Indiana Dunes Visitor Center. Staff can provide beach details; a schedule of ranger-guided walks and activities; hiking, biking and birding maps; and general information on the area.

In Focus

ZAKZEINERT/SHUTTERSTOCK ©

The Parks Today

The Great Lakes and the Midwest are home to some of the continent's most diverse reserves, from the otherworldly Badlands to tiny historic Gateway Arch. Despite a recent infusion of federal cash, the national parks face significant challenges from record-breaking visitor numbers and climate change, with more powerful storms, higher temperatures and rising sea levels causing widespread havoc.

Great American Outdoors Act

In 2020 the US Congress passed the Great American Outdoors Act, which allocated $9.5 billion over five years to national parks, forests, wildlife refuges and other federal lands. It also set aside $900 million to the Land & Water Conservation fund, which can be used to purchase additional park land. The money was desperately needed. Park attendance has increased by 50% since 1980, though the operating budget of the national park service has remained relatively flat. The backlog on much-needed repairs is staggering.

Some $10 million was needed in Voyageurs for maintenance on docks, trails, campsites and historic structures. South Dakota faced an even bigger inventory of deferred maintenance. The state listed $47 million for road repairs, building and housing improve-

ments and trail upkeep for the Badlands, Wind Cave, Mount Rushmore and other national park sites.

Ravages of Climate Change

Climate change threatens every national park in the US. Devastating fires, floods and deadly temperatures have become regular occurrences, and some parks face an existential crisis (Glacial National Park without glaciers, Joshua Tree without its eponymous trees). One of the country's most iconic parks took a huge hit in 2022, when record flooding and landslides destroyed a pivotal access road into Yellowstone.

In Cuyahoga, greater precipitation has led to increasing run-off, washing away the river's banks and causing more devastating floods. More powerful storms and rising water levels have eroded the southern shores of Lake Michigan, with Indiana Dunes seeing a 5ft rise in water levels since 2014. High water levels even led to the closure of much of Voyageurs National Park, which experienced historic flooding in 2022. Rising temperatures have also impacted plant and animal life. Milder winters has meant fewer days below freezing, which in turn has allowed invasive species to survive and spread.

The Only Options Are RAD

In 2021, the NPS published a new set of guidelines with the title Resist-Accept-Direct. These aim to give park rangers and superintendents a new framework for dealing with rapidly occurring ecological changes. This might mean planting non-native species to help the park survive higher temperatures or adding extra bends to a river to allow for heavier rainfall. Given the lack of resources, many managers may be unable to Resist or Direct change, and instead will have to Accept it, allowing ecosystems to drift into new, unprecedented scenarios, often with uncertain consequences.

Loved to Death

Many of America's national parks continue to draw record-breaking crowds. After a brief downturn during the early months of the COVID-19 pandemic, visitor numbers have rebounded to more than 300 million people per year. Larger crowds have placed bigger strains on the national parks, affecting everything from trail erosion to traffic congestion and pollution.

One solution proposed by the Sierra Club is to create more national parks. Apart from lessening pressure on existing sites, this would draw attention to other outstanding destinations, and protect more lands under the park system.

Cherokee Village, Tahlequah (p58)

History

The story begins over 10,000 years ago, when the ice sheets retreated and the first humans made their way through forests, along lakeshores and across sunbaked grasslands. Early nomadic peoples were followed over the centuries by mysterious mound builders, fur traders, pioneers, loggers and, more recently, nature lovers who helped safeguard these diverse landscapes for future generations.

20,000 BCE
Thick sheets of glacial ice cover a vast swath of North America.

8500 BCE
Early nomadic peoples hunt and fish along the shores of the Great Lakes. Their descendants later mine copper for tools and jewelry.

700–1200 CE
Disparate mound-building cultures emerge in the Midwest and the South. Settlements reach sizes of 20,000 or more.

Cannon, Fort Gibson (p58)

Early Peoples

In the beginning there was ice – at least as far as the land now known as New England, New York and northern parts of the USA was concerned. Roughly 20,000 years ago – just as humans were crossing the Bering land bridge from Asia into the Americas – the region was covered in glaciers, some 5000ft thick. The summit of 2300ft-high Eagle Mountain in Minnesota would have been deeply buried beneath the ice sheet surrounded by a frozen and impenetrable panorama.

As the planet warmed, the ice retreated, and around 13,000 years ago fur-clad Stone Age hunters found their way into the valleys, across boulder-strewn hillsides and over vast wetlands. There were also grassy plains where woolly mammoths roamed and pockets of coniferous forest emerged from the tundra. This landscape would change dramatically over the next 9000 years. The changing scenery brought new food sources (including deer, otter, beaver and bear), and new technologies allowed for the grinding and milling of plants, as well as storage techniques for roots and nuts.

1615	**1803**	**1803–06**
French explorer Samuel de Champlain becomes one of the first Europeans to reach the Great Lakes.	Napoleon sells the Louisiana Territory to the US, extending the nation's boundaries from the Mississippi to the Rockies.	Lewis and Clark, guided by Shoshone tribeswoman Sacagawea, travel from St Louis to the Pacific Ocean and back.

Native peoples made new discoveries – exploiting the copper deposits on Isle Royale some 4500 years ago, which they cold-hammered into knives, projectile points and ornaments. Even older artifacts have been unearthed in Wisconsin. Copper arrowheads, blades, fishhooks and axeheads, created more than 8500 years ago, attest to a little-known period of technological triumph that arose then suddenly disappeared. This early metallurgical savvy makes Native Americans among the world's first coppersmiths.

South of the Laurentide Ice Sheet, nomadic peoples lived in the region during prehistoric times, leaving behind traces of their presence that are still being discovered by archaeologists.

Among the recent finds are a 13,000-year-old campsite in present-day Michigan's southwest region. At the site was a distinct kind of chert used by Clovis people – considered by some scholars to be the first humans to live in the Americas. These stone tips were used in projectiles to hunt now-extinct mastodon, mammoths and giant bison along likely animal migration paths.

Mound Builders

Beginning around 2000 years ago, various distinct cultures called the Mound Builders created earthen structures in the Great Lakes region, Ohio River Valley and the Mississippi River Valley.

These flat-topped pyramid-like structures reached heights of 100ft and were up to 700ft wide at the base. They were largely used as burial chambers for important members of the local tribe, or for ceremonial purposes. Some groups also built Effigy Mounds – enormous structures in the shape of mammals, birds and reptiles. Some scholars compare these mounds to massive geoglyphs like the Nazca Lines in Peru. Though many mounds have been destroyed since Native Americans were driven off their lands, some 200 are protected as part of Effigy Mounds National Monument near the Mississippi River in northeastern Iowa.

Sizable settlements surrounded these mounds. The largest was at Cahokia, in present-day Illinois, where as many 30,000 people lived. These cultures largely reached their peak around 1200, though some mound-building tribes were still around when the Europeans arrived.

Voyageurs & the Fur Trade

French-Canadian fur traders were among the first non-Native peoples to the Great Lakes, when they began operations in the early 1600s. The demand for beaver pelts in Europe coupled with the near eradication of the animal in the east spurred the development of more distant trade routes. Each year, adventurous mostly male *voyageurs* (travelers) in crews of four to six arrived in the region shortly after the lakes thawed. They came aboard

1838–1839	1862	1865
Settlers push Native American tribes westward, often forcibly, as on the notorious Trail of Tears.	President Lincoln signs the Homestead Act. It gives out 160-acre land parcels that open up much of the US to settlement.	After four years of bloody fighting in the Civil War, the South surrenders. The final group of enslaved people is freed on June 19.

huge birchbark *canots* (canoes), which were typically 20ft to 25ft long and weighed over 250lb.

They journeyed for several months each way to reach settlements of the Ojibwe and Dakota, the main trappers of fur-bearing animals in the north. The Voyageurs traded firearms, ammunition, kettles and other metal goods along with cloth, blankets and even items they gathered along the way from other Native American communities. In exchange they received vast bales of fur that contained not only beaver hides but also the pelts of deer, muskrat and bear. Business flourished until the mid-1800s when demand for fur (and its availability) plummeted.

The *voyageurs* played a pivotal role in developing trade routes through the north, which were later used by the government in westward expansion.

Westward Expansion

In 1803, the US doubled in size virtually overnight when Napoleon sold Thomas Jefferson a vast swath of the continent as part of the Louisiana Purchase. The sale encompassed some 828,000 sq miles of land west of the Mississippi, including much of present-day Minnesota and the Dakotas, along with Missouri and many other states. This kicked off westward expansion as settlers flooded into new parts of the US.

The land of course was not empty and free for the taking. And so, over the next century, the American government would set about systematically dispossessing indigenous peoples of their lands. They would do so by treaty and by force – sometimes by open warfare.

The Indian Removal Act, signed by President Andrew Jackson in 1830, led to the forced expulsion of tens of thousands of Native Americans of the Chickasaw, Choctaw, Seminole, Cherokee and Creek tribes. Those who refused to go were rounded up and driven out of their homes on a forced march of over 1000 miles. Up to a quarter of them, some in chains, died along the way. This horrific episode was later described as the Trail of Tears, which is protected as a national historic trail.

Theodore Roosevelt: The Conservation President

In 1883, seven years after Custer passed through, en route to his infamous engagement with Sitting Bull's Sioux warriors, a young Theodore Roosevelt came to North Dakota's badlands to hunt. While here, he discovered a powerful love for the land. This passion informed his attitude towards conservation when he became president, and during his time in the White House, he would protect 230 million acres (930,777 sq km) of American wilderness. Under Roosevelt, five new national parks were created and the Antiquities Act was passed, enabling presidents to protect national monuments – many of which would later become parks.

The Oval Office was where he did his best work, but Roosevelt was most at home in the badlands backcountry, where he operated two ranches. The region turned from hunting

1883

Theodore Roosevelt arrives in the Badlands for the first time, builds a cabin and falls in love with the outdoors.

1900

Michigan is America's largest lumber producer. The devastation of its old-growth forests jumpstarts the conservation movement.

1933–42

President Franklin Roosevelt establishes the Civilian Conservation Corps.

Volunteering

Want to join the 300,000 people already volunteering in the national parks? Every year, volunteers contribute over 6.5 million hours of service to make these places better. To learn more about opportunities near you, visit www.volunteer.gov.

ground to healing ground when his wife and his mother died within hours of each other on Valentine's Day, 1884, and he sought sanctuary in the wilderness. After Roosevelt himself died in 1919, three years after the National Park Service was established, the region was explored as a possible park site and became the Theodore Roosevelt National Memorial Park in 1947 – the only National Memorial Park ever established. In 1978 it was reclassified as Theodore Roosevelt National Park.

Logging & the Birth of Conservation

In the early 19th century, a new industry began to emerge: logging. At first, it started out small, with selective timber cutting carried out by local landowners. Trees such as ash, poplar and cherry were cut down and sold to lumber mills in nearby towns. By the 1840s, however, industrialists saw enormous financial opportunities in the large stands of old-growth forest and began buying up properties and commencing large-scale operations.

Companies laid down railroad tracks to transport timber, built large mills and created lumber towns that grew into sizable villages. Hundreds of miles of logging roads were blazed through the forests. Logging boom towns arrived overnight. By 1920, many old-growth forests were completely cut down. With no remaining timber, logging operations ground to a halt, the mills closed and nearby towns were abandoned.

As widespread felling of forests became publicized, a growing number of civic leaders called for an end to the heedless destruction. In 1901 Michigan's citizen forestry movement pressured the legislature to create the first forest reserves. The conservation movement picked up steam in the decades ahead with the creation of the US Forest Service in 1905 and the creation of National Forests beginning in 1909.

The Great Depression & the CCC

The early 1930s was a devastating period for many in the US. The stock market crash of 1929 heralded dark days ahead, with bank collapses, crop failures brought on by drought, and mass migrations of people from the countryside into the city in a desperate search for work. By 1933, more than one in four working-age Americans were unemployed.

As the Great Depression swept across the nation in the early 1930s, President Franklin Roosevelt came up with an innovative solution to put people back to work. He created the Civilian Conservation Corps, or CCC, which would serve two purposes: it would create jobs and it would help in the nation's reforestation. CCC camps were set up across the country,

1950
Secretary of the Interior, Harold Ickes, desegregates the National Park Service.

1966
Conservationists win a victory over industrialists as Congress designates the Indiana Dunes a national lakeshore.

1996
Robert Stanton becomes the first African American Director of the NPS.

including in numerous national-park sites. Over the course of its existence, over three million people – mostly young men – worked for the corps, which ran from 1933 to 1942. They labored at a variety of jobs: constructing access roads and bridges, planting trees, blazing trails and building water systems and other essential park infrastructure. Some groups were even charged with raising trout to replenish fish-depleted streams.

The arrival of WWII brought an end to the CCC, the country's greatest public relief program. The camps were closed down and many became abandoned ghost towns amid the quickly encroaching forest. The forest workers went off to war, and the national park budget was slashed.

Evolution of the Parks

The parks have undergone changes – some subtle, others seismic – since their early days. Cramped visitor centers that were once little more than dark chambers full of dusty taxidermy animals and uninspiring natural history have been transformed into modern, sustainably designed buildings aimed at accommodating a wide range of visitors, including those with disabilities.

Parks are also aiming to increase diversity – both among staff and visitors. For many years, park ranger jobs were the exclusive domain of men. Things slowly began changing in 1964 after the passage of title VII of the Civil Rights Act, which made it unlawful to discriminate against someone on the basis of race, color, national origin, sex or religion. Over the next decade, more women joined the NPS, though the female uniform (with stewardess-like miniskirts and tunics, plus optional go-go boots) wasn't retired until 1978. These days around 37% of park service employees are women, which some former employees describe (along with reports of sexism, sexual harassment and even assault) as indicative of how the NPS is failing women.

Minorities have long been under-represented in national parks. African Americans make up under 7% of the park's permanent full-time workforce, despite making up over 13% of the US population. Similarly, less than 6% of the NPS workforce are Latinos, despite composing nearly 19% of the population. Visitors are also overwhelmingly white. This is perhaps not surprising given the history of racism and discrimination that people of color faced when attempting to visit national park sites. Even once segregation ended at the park, Black visitors still had to get there, contending with segregated restaurants, hotels and restaurants along the way. Meanwhile, at all 150 state parks that opened during the Great Depression in the south, African Americans were simply denied entry.

Rather than sweep history under the rug, the NPS admits it has work to do. Leaders like Robert Stanton, who was the first and only African American Director of the Park Service, have served as role models for future generations, and the service continues to strategize about new ways to attract people of color to national parks, which belong to all Americans.

2015	**2018**	**2020**
President Obama launches an initiative that gives a free annual national-parks pass to fourth graders and their families.	The Gateway Arch in St Louis becomes the US's 60th and smallest national park, measuring just 191 acres.	Great American Outdoors Act allocates up to $1.9 billion annually for five years to national-park maintenance and conservation.

ELLEN CHARIS PHOTOGRAPHY/SHUTTERSTOCK ©

Outdoor Activities

Mountains, coasts and forests set the stage for an array of adventures. Scramble up striated plateaus to magnificent views over the Badlands or paddle along crystalline lakes in the Boundary Waters. Cycle along wooded paths in Cuyahoga and rock-climb up granite spires. During the off season, enjoy crowd-free trails and enchanting wintery backdrops on snowshoes or cross-country skis.

Hiking

Nothing encapsulates the spirit of the national parks like hiking. Thousands of miles of trails criss-cross the parks, offering access to rocky summits, crystal-clear lakes, thundering waterfalls and tranquil corners amid old-growth forests. Trails run the gamut of accessibility, from flat, fully accessible trails along the **Ohio & Erie Canal Towpath** in the Cuyahoga Valley to the thrilling 111-mile **Centennial Trail** through the Black Hills.

Regardless of the style of the trail, you'll find that exploring on foot generally offers the best park experience. The relatively slow pace of walking brings you into closer contact with the wildlife, and allows you to appreciate the way different perspectives and the day's shifting light can alter the scenery. The satisfaction gained from completing a hike is also a worthy reward; it's one thing to look over the rim of the Grand Canyon, it's another to work up a sweat hiking back up from the canyon floor.

Throughout this guide, you'll find a variety of trails. Our goal with descriptions is less about navigation than it is about helping you choose which hikes to squeeze into your trip. Detailed trail descriptions and maps are readily available at visitor centers in every park, and they will complement this guide well. Know your limitations, know the route you plan to take and pace yourself.

Backpacking

There are hundreds of amazing day hikes to choose from in the park system, but if you want the full experience, head out into the wilderness on an overnight trip. The claim that 99% of park visitors never make it into the backcountry may not be true everywhere, but you will unquestionably see far fewer people and witness exponentially more magic the further from a road you go. Backcountry campsites are also much more likely to have openings than park lodges and car campsites (which fill up months in advance), making accommodations less of a headache.

Even if you have no backpacking experience, don't consider it out of reach. Most national parks have at least a few backcountry campsites within a couple of hours' walk of a trailhead, making them excellent options for first-time backpackers. You will need gear, however: an appropriate backpack, tent, sleeping bag and pad, headlamp and food are all essential – as is a stove and fuel if you plan on hot meals.

Familiarize yourself with the park rules and backcountry ethics before heading out. You will need a permit; if you have your heart set on a famous excursion, apply online well in advance. Most park visitor centers have a backcountry desk, where you can apply for walk-in permits, get trail information, learn about wildlife (bear canisters or suspension bags for hanging food are generally required) and check conditions. Before hitting the trail, learn about low-impact camping principles at Leave No Trace (lnt.org).

Open Hike Parks

The **Badlands National Park** is one of several open hike parks out west. This means you can walk and camp anywhere you like as long as you pitch your tent at least half a mile away from any roads or trails.

In a reserve that encompasses 381 sq miles, the biggest challenge will be deciding where to begin. Good backcountry settings include Sage Creek where you can often spot bison. West of the Conata picnic area, you can hike along towering buttes, set up camp overlooking the prairie, in a juniper grove or on a clifftop — all magnificent places to absorb the quiet beauty of this rugged wilderness.

Preparation & Safety

Walks can be as short or long as you like, but remember this when planning: be prepared. The wilderness may be unlike anything you have ever experienced, and designating certain parcels 'national parks' has not tamed it.

The weather can be extraordinary in its unpredictability and sheer force. The summer sun is blazing hot, sudden thunderstorms can drop enough water in 10 minutes to create deadly flash floods, heavy snowfalls are a possibility even in spring, while ferocious wind storms can rip or blow away your poorly staked tent.

No matter where you are, water should be the number one item on your packing checklist – always carry more than you think you'll need. If you're doing any backpacking, make sure you have a way to purify water, and check with rangers ahead of time about the availability of water along the trail.

★ **Classic Day Hikes**

Castle Trail (Badlands)

Caprock Coulee Loop (Theodore Roosevelt)

Stoll Memorial Trail (Isle Royale)

West Beach 3-Loop Trail (Indiana Dunes)

Ledges Trail (Cuyahoga Valley)

Sunblock, a hat, ibuprofen and warm windproof and waterproof layers are all essentials when hiking. After the elements, getting lost is the next major concern. Most day hikes are well signed and visitors are numerous, but you should always take some sort of map. If you plan on going into the backcountry, definitely take a topographic (topo) map and a compass. You can pick up detailed maps in most visitor centers; National Geographic's *Trails Illustrated* series is generally excellent.

Always ask about ticks, poison oak, poison ivy and venomous snakes before heading out. Most day hikes are on well-maintained trails, but it's good to know what's out there.

And all hikers, solo or not, should always remember the golden rule: let someone know where you are going and how long you plan to be gone.

Kayaking & Canoeing

The Great Lakes are a paddler's paradise, with more than 35,000 lakes spread across Michigan, Minnesota and Wisconsin.

Kayaks, canoes and larger boats are a wonderful way to get to parts of the parks that landlubbers can't reach. For epic adventures, it's hard to think of a better place than the **Boundary Waters**. The reserve has over 1200 miles of canoe routes and some 2000 designated campsites. If larger bodies of water are more your speed, one of the best parks to explore in a canoe or kayak is **Voyageurs** on the Minnesota–Canada border, which consists of over 30 lakes and 900 islands. Another northern park offering kayaking trips is **Isle Royale**, the largest island in Lake Superior. Many of the campgrounds in both of these parks are only accessible by boat.

If you prefer to go on a kayaking tour rather than going on your own, you'll find operators near Voyageurs, the Apostle Islands and Sleeping Bear Dunes National Lakeshore, among other places.

Canoe Trip Preparation

It's possible to glide in for the day in some places, but most people opt for at least a night of camping.

Whether you're an expert or a novice, you need to be prepared for a real wilderness adventure when canoeing. Make sure you have good maps, and arrange for permits and campsite reservations (where needed) well in advance. For the Boundary Waters and Voyageurs, reserve through www.recreation.gov. For Isle Royale, you'll receive your permit on the ferry ride to the island; campsites on the island are then first come, first served.

You can rent canoes and other gear at a gateway town. For the Boundary Waters, head to Ely (pronounced EE-lee), which has excellent outfitters and scores of accommodations and restaurants.

Boat Tours

Access to some parts of the Great Lakes is only possible by boat or ferry, and many of these services also double as boat tours. The National Park Service at **Voyageurs** offers trips ranging from one-hour jaunts to full-day excursions. Highlights include the former gold mine on Little American Island, Kettle Falls and the Ellsworth Rock Gardens. You might also see beavers, bears, bald eagles and other wildlife. Tours depart from Rainy Lake Visitor Center and Kabetogama Lake Visitor Center primarily from June through August. Private outfits also run tours, including fishing trips.

Further south, boat tours take in the beauty of the **Apostle Islands**. Popular excursions like the 'grand tour' take you past sea caves, lighthouses and dense island forests on narrated three-hour tours. You can also book a tour by glass-bottom boat, which goes out to view shipwrecks just off the islands.

Houseboats

Unlike Minnesota's Boundary Waters Canoe Area Wilderness, which is directly east, in Voyageurs motorized boats are allowed, which makes the park more accessible to families, and folks who may not want to heft a canoe from lake to lake. Outfitters like Voyagaire (www. voyagaire.com) rent out houseboats that sleep from four to 12, and come fully equipped with bathrooms and kitchen units. The biggest craft even has an eight-person hot tub. No prior experience is necessary to operate the boats. All you need is a driver's license.

Rock Climbing

There's no sport quite like rock climbing. From a distance it appears to be a feat of sheer strength, but balance, creativity, technical know-how and a Zen-like sangfroid are all parts of the game. A top destination for rock climbers is the **Black Hills**. Granite towers, pillars and spires have a mix of routes for both beginners and more experienced climbers.

Less than an hour's drive north of there, **Mt Rushmore** also has some excellent granite rock-climbing routes, though you won't be dangling from Lincoln's nose a la Cary Grant in *North by Northwest* since climbing on the president isn't allowed. Custer-based Sylvan Rocks (www.sylvanrocks.com) leads climbing excursions ranging from four to eight hours.

Cycling & Mountain Biking

As a general rule, expect more options for two-wheeled fun just outside park boundaries. There are, however, some exceptions. The **Maah Daah Hey Trail**, which links the north and south units of Theodore Roosevelt National Park, is one of the great multi-day single-track routes in the US. You'll pass through some dramatic sections of the Badlands along the way with opportunities for wildlife-watching. Speaking of Badlands, the South Dakota national park has some fine routes along gravel roads, including the 23-mile **Sage Creek Loop** where you might spot bighorn sheep, prairie dogs and bison.

At Indiana Dunes, an interconnected trail system encompasses 37 miles (60km) across the national park, and takes in towering dunes, prairie and forested stretches. Memorable jaunts include the 2.1-mile **Marquette Trail** and the 10.3-mile **Prairie-Duneland Trail**, both take in ponds, dunes and woodlands along an abandoned rail line.

In Cuyahoga, around 20 miles of the historic 87-mile **Ohio and Erie Canal Towpath** passes through the park, and cycling it has become a must-do experience.

★ **Classic Backcountry Trips**

Maah Daah Hey Trail (Theodore Roosevelt)

Cruiser Lake Trail (Voyageurs)

Greenstone Ridge Trail (Isle Royale)

Big Carp River Trail (Porcupine Mountains Wilderness State Park)

North Country Trail (Pictured Rocks National Lakeshore)

Winter Sports

Cross-Country Skiing & Snowshoeing

Come winter, trails and roads in many parks get blanketed with snow and the crowds disappear. It's a magical time to visit, and those willing to step into skis or snowshoes and brave the elements will be rewarded. For many winter-loving northerners, this is the best time of year.

In many places in the north snow can arrive in late October and stick around until April. At some places you'll have to blaze your own ski trails, though you'll sometimes find surprising alternatives. At **Theodore Roosevelt**, for instance, the frozen Little Missouri River and the closed (to traffic) park roads are great places for cross-country skiing.

In the winter at **Voyageurs**, frozen lakes transform into ice roads – such as the link between the boat launches of the Ash River and Kabetogama Lake Visitor Center. This gives road access to otherwise inaccessible islands during the coldest months, which you can then explore by snowshoe or cross-country skis. Young visitors often love the thrill of speeding down the Sphunge Island-Kabetogama Lake Sledding Hill. Voyageurs loans out essential gear to winter visitors – with snowshoe and ski sizes, along with boots and poles for both kids and adults.

Indiana Dunes is another good spot for snowshoeing and skiing. You can rent gear from the Paul H Douglas Center for Environmental Education for use on the Paul H Douglas Trail, but for other trails (all ungroomed), you'll need to arrive with your own gear.

Sleeping Bear Dunes has groomed sections of the Sleeping Bear Heritage Trail for skiing. Other trails are not groomed though some are designated as ski trails. Snowshoers head to the park's dunes, forests and fields. The dunes are also great for sledding.

In some of these parks, rangers lead snowshoe hikes, which can be an excellent entry to the sport and a great way to learn about the winter environment. Visitor centers are the best place to check for information.

Swimming

When the summer heat arrives, you can cool off in lakes, gurgling streams and waterfall-fed natural pools. As river rats the world over will attest, nothing beats dipping into a swimming hole and drip-drying on a rock in the sun. But be careful – every year swimmers drown in national park rivers. Always check with visitor centers about trouble spots and the safest places to swim. Unless you're certain about the currents, swim only where others are swimming.

Some shorelines on the Great Lakes can resemble ocean seascapes, with sandy beaches and gently lapping waves. It's worth planning a trip around lovely spots like **Sleeping Bear Dunes** and **Indiana Dunes**, which have enticing beaches for a swim. Keep in mind that swimming in any of the Great Lakes is a chilly endeavor – which can be the perfect antidote to a sweltering 90°F (35°C) day in July.

Fishing

For many, the idea of heading to the national parks without a fishing rod is ludicrous. You can find picturesque streams and rivers all across the region, along with the legendary fishing in the Great Lakes themselves. The big draws are steelhead, two types of salmon (Coho, Chinook), various species of trout (lake trout, brown trout, rainbow trout) as well as smallmouth bass, largemouth bass and walleye.

In winter, many fishers don't put away their rods for the season, they just go ice fishing instead. You can join them at many places across the region, including the lakes in **Custer State Park**, where you can fish for trout and crappie. Hardcore winter fishers even set up ice houses on the lakes of **Voyageurs**.

Wherever you fish, read up on local regulations. Fishing permits are always required, and those caught fishing without one will be fined. (Children under 16 are generally not required to have a license.) Some waters, including many streams and rivers, are catch-and-release only, and sometimes bait-fishing is prohibited. Certain native fish are often protected, and anglers in possession of these can be heavily fined. The best place to check regulations is online. For details on regulations, check the park's NPS website on Fish & Fishing (www.nps.gov/subjects/fishing/fishing.htm).

Alternative Adventures

You'll find plenty of less common ways to experience these wild landscapes. A few ideas for a memorable outing:

○ **Stargazing** You'll find outstanding spots across the region, especially in the Badlands. Also check park newspapers for nightly astronomy walks.

○ **Surfing** Believe it or not, there's great surf to be had in the Great Lakes. Sleeping Bear Dunes National Lakeshore is a prime spot.

○ **Caving** Head to Wind Cave, which offers a variety of subterranean tours, including a half-day spelunking adventure with helmets, kneepads and headlamps included.

○ **Train spotting** You can ride the rails or watch the Cuyahoga Valley Scenic Railroad (CVSR) chug past in Ohio's national park.

○ **Fruit picking** Grab a basket and pick strawberries, apples, pumpkins and other seasonal fruit at Center Grove Orchard in the Silos and Smokestacks National Heritage Area.

Horseback Riding

Our most time-tested form of transport still makes for a wonderful way to experience the great outdoors. The Great Lakes have limited opportunities for horseback, though as you go west or south, you'll find some spectacular settings for a trail ride. Among the best destinations is the **Black Hills** of South Dakota, where you can ride through canyons, mixed-grass prairies, up wooded slopes and along lofty ridgelines. Rides run around $50 per hour or $90 per half-day.

Wildlife Watching

Beyond the big cities of the Midwest, black bears still roam through primeval forests and the plaintive howls of a coyote pierce the night sky. The national parks and reserves reconnect you to the wild world of our ancestors. Whether you're on the trail of moose in Minnesota or stumbling upon prairie dog towns in the Dakotas, the power of nature is all around you.

White-Tailed Deer

One animal that most visitors see is the white-tailed deer, which can be spotted in forested areas all across the region. Tan or reddish brown in color, the white-tailed deer weighs between 100lb and 200lb (males can weigh up to 300lb). White-tailed deer can run fast, reaching speeds up to 40mph, and can jump distances of up to 30ft.

Only the bucks (males) have antlers. These regrow each year, beginning in late spring and summer when they are covered in a protective hairlike membrane called 'velvet'. The antlers harden by fall, when bucks use them to fight and establish dominance over other males during the breeding season. Does (females) give birth about six months after mating, and have between one and three fawns. These are reddish brown in color with white spots that help camouflage them in sun-dappled forests.

The best time to spot deer is when they're foraging and feeding, in the early morning and late afternoon. Deer sometimes wander across roads in forested areas. Be especially vigilant when driving between dusk and dawn, and don't speed.

Bison, Moose & Other Grazers

The continent's largest land mammal is the **American bison** (or buffalo). Some 60 million bison once roamed North America, but Euro-American settlers, in one of the saddest chapters of American history, reduced their numbers to about 300. Beginning in the 1860s, the US government and army encouraged the slaughter in order to deprive the Plains Indians of their primary means of survival.

What could have been a disaster instead became a turning point. Thanks to the determined intervention of George Bird Grinnell, editor of *Forest & Stream* and founder of the Audubon Society, and a young politician by the name of Theodore Roosevelt, Congress passed an 1894 law granting national parks the power to protect all wildlife within their boundaries. Previous to this, poachers were simply expelled from park lands; now they could be arrested. Today, you'll find a herd numbering about 450 in Badlands National Parks, and an even larger population in Custer State Park.

Other large grazers are present in some parks. **Moose**, the largest of the world's deer species, stand 5ft to 7ft at the shoulder and can weigh up to 1000lb. An estimated 4000 moose live in Minnesota, along with tiny populations in Wisconsin and Michigan.

The Dakotas have a few unique species you won't spot elsewhere in the region. **Elk** grow antlers up to 5ft long and weigh up to 700lb. These majestic herbivores graze along forest edges and are commonly sighted.

Bighorn sheep are sometimes spotted on rocky precipices in the Badlands. During late-fall and early-winter breeding seasons, males charge each other at 20mph and clash their horns so powerfully that the sound can be heard for miles.

Though not native to the area, the fuzzy sure-footed **mountain goats**, actually a species of antelope, have lived in the Black Hills since the 1920s. In the open prairies of the Badlands, you might spy **pronghorn antelope**, North America's fastest land animal, capable of reaching speeds of 55mph.

Black Bears

Up to 6ft long, and standing 3ft high at the shoulder, the American black bear is the symbol of the US Forest Service. Males typically weigh around 250lb (females around 100lb), though bears weighing up to 600lb have been found. Sizable populations live in Michigan, Wisconsin and Minnesota (each with over 12,000 bears), though there is almost no presence in the lower Midwest.

Though they look like lumbering creatures when they walk, black bears can run fast, reaching speeds of up to 30mph. Black bears are omnivores and subsist on wild berries, acorns, grasses, tree buds, flowers and roots, with plant materials providing about 85% of their diet. The other 15% comes from insects, animal carrion and other sources of protein.

Black bears have better eyesight and hearing than humans, though their strongest sense is smell, which is about seven times keener than a dog's. They are most active in the early-morning and late-evening hours during the spring and summer. In the wild, bears live an average of 12 to 15 years.

Contrary to common belief, black bears are not true hibernators but do enter long periods of sleep. They may emerge from their winter dens periodically during unusually warm spells or if they are disturbed. Female bears sometimes have a surprise waiting for them when they awaken in the springtime, as their offspring are born during their winter sleep.

★ Best Wildlife Sightings

Moose (Isle Royale)

Elk and bighorn sheep (Badlands)

Bison (Custer State Park)

Gray wolf (Voyageurs)

Bald eagles (Pictured Rocks National Lakeshore)

Prairie Dogs (Theodore Roosevelt)

Females typically give birth to one to four cubs every other year. The cubs arrive in January or February. These tiny newborns weigh just 10oz (less than a can of soda) and will remain close to the mother for about 18 months, or until she mates again. Mating, incidentally, typically takes place in July. Both male and female bears have more than one mate during the summer. Black bears are usually not aggressive unless there are cubs nearby, but they will go after food or food odors. Make sure to store your food and trash properly, and hang food using a bear bag if you plan on backpacking.

Wolves

The wolf is a potent symbol of America's wilderness. This smart, adaptable predator is the largest species of canine – averaging more than 100lb and reaching nearly 3ft at the shoulder. Highly social animals, they live in small packs of four to eight individuals and work together to bring down large animals like moose.

Wolves were not regarded warmly by European settlers. The first wildlife legislation in the British colonies was a wolf bounty. And as 19th-century Americans moved west, they replaced the native herds of bison, elk, deer and moose with domestic cattle and sheep, which wolves found equally tasty. To stop wolves from devouring the livestock, extermination soon became official government policy. Up until 1965, for $20 to $50 an animal, wolves were shot, poisoned, trapped and dragged from dens, until in the Lower 48 states only a few hundred gray wolves remained, in northern Minnesota and Michigan.

In 1944 naturalist Aldo Leopold called for the return of the wolf. His argument was ecology, not nostalgia. His studies showed that wild ecosystems need their top predators to maintain healthy biodiversity; in complex interdependence, all animals and plants suffered with the wolf gone.

Protected and encouraged, wolf populations have made a remarkable recovery. In Minnesota the wolf population had plummeted to less than 350 wolves in the 1960s. Now there are more than 2500 individuals in the state. The neighboring states of Michigan and Wisconsin have witnessed similar recoveries. Where virtually none existed 50 years ago, there are now more than 900 wolves in Wisconsin and some 700 wolves living in Michigan's Upper Peninsula. The best time to spot them is at dawn or dusk.

Coyotes

Coyotes have a wiry build with sandy-brown fur, bushy tails and upright ears. They resemble a medium-sized dog and rarely grow above 40lb. Intelligent and highly adaptable, coyotes are omnivores, eating birds, rabbits and other small prey, as well as plants, fruits and carrion. You may not see a coyote, but you can look for its presence. Its footprints reveal large pads with four toes tipped with evident claws at the end of each appendage.

If you camp in a park, you might also hear the soulful howl of a coyote. In autumn and winter, this normally solitary creature gathers in small packs for more effective hunting.

Now present throughout much of America, coyotes are relatively recent arrivals to the region. After wolves disappeared owing to overhunting and habitat loss, the highly adaptable coyote filled the ecological niche of its bigger canine relatives. Filling this hole in the ecosystem means that they aren't considered an invasive species.

Cats

North America's largest cat is the **mountain lion** (also known as a puma or cougar), an elusive and powerful predator. Adult males can measure over 7ft nose to tail and weigh up to 220lb, though they are usually smaller. More common out west, mountain lions have a small presence in the Black Hills, with an estimated population of around 300. Bafflingly, South Dakota allow trophy hunters to kill these impressive felines, with a quota of up to 60 males or 40 females each year. Populations are clearly declining, with fewer lions harvested each successive year between 2013 and 2022.

It's highly unlikely you'll spot one, as they avoid human contact. If you're camping, however, you may hear one scream – it's an utterly terrifying sound in the darkness and a virtual guarantee that you won't fall back asleep until dawn.

Bobcats are also present in some of these parks. True to name, bobcats have short, stumpy tails and can weigh up to 70lb. These solitary creatures, with their spotted fur and tufted ears, are quite striking, though rarely spotted owing to their nocturnal habits. **Lynx** are rarer still as they prefer the dense arboreal forests of Canada and are specialist hunters that prey primarily on the snowshoe hare. They are occasionally spotted in northern Minnesota and Michigan's Upper Peninsula.

Wolf vs Moose

The helicopter swooped low along the edge of the snow-covered forest. As the wolf darted out across the frozen lake, the pilot banked in pursuit. The crew fired the netgun and ensnared the bounding animal. While lying entangled, the wolf was tranquilized, then loaded into the helicopter and carried off. After checking its health at a veterinary station, the apex predator continued its journey to a new home: Isle Royale. She would be the first of some 19 wolves brought to the island between 2018 and 2020.

Since 1958, researchers on Isle Royale have been conducting the world's longest-running study of a predator-prey system: exploring the delicate connection between wolves and moose, and learning about the surprising repercussions when nature was out of balance. As the wolf population plummeted and the moose population soared, the whole ecosystem was affected as overgrazing destroyed plant diversity and impacted other animals (like snowshoe hares) that rely on the same food source.

With just two wolves left on the island by 2016, the park settled on a radical solution: they would reintroduce new wolves taken from other parts of Michigan, Minnesota and Ontario in hopes of bringing equilibrium to Isle Royale. So far, the results are promising. New wolf pups have been born on the island, and the moose population has stabilized.

Beavers

Nearly everyone's favorite rodent is the North American beaver. Described by scientists as a 'keystone' species, beavers are vital, and without them an ecosystem can collapse. They are also prolific builders, gnawing through trees and branches, which they carry between their teeth. Combining the timber with mud and small stones, beavers build dams and lodges – feats of engineering that have a profound affect on the landscape.

By blocking streams, they flood the surrounding forest, which creates an ideal environment to raise their young – lodges are only accessible by underwater entrance, a strong deterrent to predators. The newly-formed ponds benefit plant and animal life, with some tree species (like the willow) flourishing from the abundant water source.

Beavers can grow 2ft long and typically weigh between 30lb and 60lb. They are excellent swimmers and can see well underwater, though they have relatively poor eyesight on land. They can also hold their breath for up to 15 minutes. Beavers mate for life and each lodge contains a pair of adults and their offspring (kits).

Before the arrival of winter, beavers store up tree bark and roots to get them through the months when other food sources are scarce. At other times of year, they feed on aquatic plants as well as forest fruits and berries.

Prairie Dogs

Despite the name, prairie dogs have nothing in common with canines. Members of the Sciuridae family, they are related to squirrels and chipmunks, and reside all across the Great Plains. These highly social animals live in vast underground colonies, called 'towns', that offer protection from predators and flash floods. Like beavers, prairie dogs are a keystone species and play an important role in the health of the ecosystem. Look for them on the Loop Rd in Badlands.

Birds of Prey

Birds of prey – including eagles, falcons, hawks, owls and harriers – are common in the parks, with several dozen species present.

The bald eagle was adopted as the nation's symbol in 1782. It's the only eagle unique to North America, and perhaps half a million once ruled the continent's skies. By 1963, habitat destruction and, in particular, poisoning from DDT had caused the population to plummet to 487 breeding pairs in the lower 48 states. By 2007, however, bald eagles had recovered so well, increasing to almost 9800 breeding pairs across the continent, that they were removed from the endangered species list. Nowadays, they are found in every state apart from Hawaii, with an estimated 300,000 in the US.

Peregrine falcons also nest here and, like bald eagles, have made a remarkable comeback since the 1970s. The world's fastest animal, peregrine falcons can reach speeds of up to 180mph when diving for prey from lofty heights. Osprey, which nest and hunt around rivers and lakes, are another commonly spotted raptor.

Aquatic Birds

Lakes and ponds provide key habitats for some species, including the iconic common loon. These black-and-white plumed birds, with their distinctive red eyes, are known for their haunting calls. Though their numbers reached record lows by the 1970s, their population has stabilized in recent years. Minnesota has more loons (over 12,000) than any state except Alaska.

Badlands National Park

EQROY/SHUTTERSTOCK ©

Conservation

Protecting America's wild spaces has been a challenge since Teddy Roosevelt first fell in love with the Badlands back in the 1880s. Thanks to the efforts of passionate individuals, the parks now safeguard some of the greatest natural treasures on the planet. But they face new, often concurrent, threats. Climate change, invasive species and pollution all jeopardize the national parks today.

Climate Change

Major voices within the National Parks Service, in agreement with scores of eminent scientists and climatologists, know that climate change poses a significant threat to the health of the network's diverse ecosystems. Although park biologists are only just beginning to understand the impact of climate change, nearly all agree that it's taking a toll.

Climate change has caused warmer waters, more precipitation and fiercer storms. This has led to coastal erosion, not only on America's oceanfronts, but also on its lakeshores. Indiana Dunes has seen its worst erosion in history, with beaches as well as some infrastructure disappearing into the lake. Warmer weather has also meant less ice covering the shores during the lake's colder months and less protection from strong winter storms.

Invasive Species

Invasive species pose a severe threat to the national parks. In Cuyahoga Valley, some 61 non-native species are invading the park. Japanese knotweed, which can grow up to 10ft high, has taken over the understory of some forests, preventing new trees from maturing. It also leads to erosion on the riverbanks. This is particularly alarming given that the noxious plant covers an estimated 40% of the riverbanks along the park's 26 miles of the Cuyahoga River. The recent appearance of zebra mussels in Voyageurs has led to intense efforts to control its spread. These creatures can lead to the extinction of native mollusks and imperil native fish as food sources are reduced.

The seemingly innocuous yellow sweet clover is an invader of the Badlands. As it and other non-native species spread across the prairie, they can out-compete native grasses that bison and many other herbivores rely on for survival. Of course, we can hardly remove ourselves from the list of invasive species. Each year millions of visitors travel to and through the parks. Traffic, roads, encroaching development and the simple fact of human presence in sensitive wildlife areas all take their toll on park ecosystems.

Pollution

Aside from the impact visitors make on the parks, humans are putting immense pressure on many parks in the Great Lakes and the Midwest owing to carbon emissions from big cities, heavy industry and the abundance of cars and trucks. Coal-fired plants in the Midwest continue to be among the nation's biggest polluters when it comes to energy production. Michigan and other states bordering the lakes also have power plants that release toxic metals into the Great Lakes and other waterways. Even places where you wouldn't expect to find pollution – like the Badlands – sometimes suffer from poor air quality owing to nearby oil and gas production, as well as distant coal plants that can cause visible air pollution.

Sustainable Visitation

As magnificent as they are, national park sites receive only a tiny percentage of the US national budget, and have often struggled to get adequate funding. The $9.5-billion Great American Outdoors Act, passed in 2020, will address long-deferred maintenance – though much more is needed to ensure the viability of the parks in the decades ahead. Visitors can also make a positive impact by traveling sustainably and getting involved with park associations.

Whenever you can, ride park shuttles or hop on a bike instead of driving your car. Skip high-impact park activities such as helicopter flights over Badlands or big bus tours around St Louis. Prevent erosion by always staying on trails. If you're backpacking, use biodegradable soaps (or skip them altogether) and follow the principles of Leave No Trace (lnt.org).

Nearly every site run by the NPS has an associated foundation or other non-profit that supports its parent park. These organizations, which include Voyageurs Conservancy (www.voyageurs.org), Friends of Indiana Dunes (www.dunefriends.org) and Conservancy for Cuyahoga Valley National Park (www.conservancyforcvnp.org) conduct everything from trail maintenance and shoreline cleanups to habitat restoration. Members can volunteer or donate to programs that are critical to the parks' well-being.

The National Parks Conservation Association (www.npca.org) covers all of the parks. Since 1919 this nonprofit organization has been protecting and preserving America's national parks through research, advocacy and education.

WIN-INITIATIVE/GETTY IMAGES ©

★ Did you know?

More than 200 national parks and monuments contain at least one endangered species.

BOTTOM LEFT: ED RESCHKE/GETTY IMAGES ©; BOTTOM RIGHT: AB PHOTOGRAPHIE/SHUTTERSTOCK ©

Top: Mountain yellow-legged frog
Left: Black tail prairie dog
Bottom right: Grey wolf

Abandoned prairie shack, South Dakota

GUNTHER ALLEN/SHUTTERSTOCK ©

Landscapes & Geology

The powerful forces of nature have created some of North America's most dramatic landscapes, from the world's biggest freshwater lake system to ancient canyons full of 300-million-year-old fossils. You'll find verdant forests, massive dunes and windswept prairies – all supporting a complex array of ecosystems. Learn the story behind the landscapes to add greater depth to your travels.

The Ice Age

Around two million years ago the earth entered a cold spell (aka the Pleistocene Epoch) and plunging temperatures initiated the Great Ice Age. Glacial ice marched across the continent (and across huge swaths of the globe), melted, then advanced once again over at least a dozen different periods. As glaciers flowed over the landscape, they eroded mountains, carved deep valleys and even altered the geography of the Ohio River and other waterways.

The final episode happened around 20,000 years ago during the so-called Wisconsin Glaciation. That's when the ice sheets reached their maximum extent, growing up to one mile thick and stretching across millions of square miles. All of present-day Michigan and

Minnesota were covered by glaciers, along with much of the Dakotas, Wisconsin and other states in the Midwest.

The Great Lakes

When the climate warmed, the ice retreated, revealing a dramatically transformed landscape. Huge deposits (including cobbles, sand, clay and silt) were left behind along with boulders (aka glacial erratics), sometimes strewn miles away from their origin. The end of the Ice Age also saw the emergence of inland 'seas': five freshwater lakes of such gargantuan size that they practically constitute a fourth US coastline.

There are more than 9500 miles of shoreline, longer than the East Coast and the Gulf Coast combined. The lakes also contain some 35,000 islands. Water is in astonishing abundance: together the five lakes make up the largest freshwater system on earth, some 6 quadrillion gallons – 90% of America's freshwater and 20% of the world's freshwater. If spread evenly across the continental US, the entire country would be submerged beneath nearly 9.5ft of water.

Aside from abundant H_2O, this region is home to the largest freshwater coastal wetlands. These support a variety of plant and animal life – from web-footed muskrats to lumbering moose – along with diverse ecosystems that include freshwater estuaries, marshes, bogs, lake prairies and dunes. These wetlands play a crucial role in helping to clean and improve water quality and reduce flooding.

The terrain around the lakes is quite diverse. Multi-colored sandstone cliffs, some reaching heights of 200ft, stretch along parts of Lake Superior (most evidently at Pictured Rocks National Lakeshore). Sea caves, blowholes, arches and spires are also among the features found here, and they are evidence of Precambrian sedimentary rocks created more than 800 million years ago.

Dunes

On other parts of the shore, the lake borders extensive dune systems. The tallest dunes are the perched dunes (those that sit atop an existing coastal bluff) west of Grand Marais, which tower some 300ft above the water line. Compared to other geological features, these dunes are relative youths. Stones left behind by the final retreat of glacial ice 10,000 years ago created the rocky bluffs. The lake waters rose and fell in this geologically tumultuous time. During a high water time, the waves lapping the shore eroded the cliffs, creating sand, which in a later low-water period were blown by offshore winds onto the tops of the bluffs where they stand today. Sleeping Bear Dune is only about 2000 years old.

Far from being static, the dunes are constantly changing. Mount Baldy, the largest 'living' dune in Indiana Dunes National Park moves inland about 4ft each year, consuming grasses, shrubs and even trees in its path. Sleeping Bear Dunes contains 'ghost forests' – the skeletons of trees that grew on the dunes when sand levels were lower; they were later buried by the onslaught of shifting sands.

These arid soils support an array of unique animal and plant life, including desert plants like the eastern prickly pear cactus. The endangered fringed polygala, which grows only on the north slope of one particular dune is found nowhere else in Indiana. Lake Superior's dunes have rare species like Lake Huron tansy and moonwort ferns.

G.L.O.A.T.

The unofficial twitter account for Lake Superior (@LakeSuperior) loves to celebrate her greatness. Though lighthearted at times – 'Without me, they would be called the Good Lakes' – Superior celebrates all things Great Lake related, from indigenous rock paintings to inspiring clifftop sunsets.

Birthplace of Ecology

The extraordinary variety of vascular plants in the differing habitats of the Indiana Dunes attracted the attention of botanist Henry Cowles in the early 1900s. Cowles and other scientists made groundbreaking studies in the newly emerging field of ecology, and put the region on the map, ultimately saving it from destruction over the next half century.

Carnivorous flora thrive here, including the purple pitcher plant, which collects rainwater in its hollow gibbous leaves, which lure (and later trap) insects. Orchids are particularly abundant. There are more orchids in Indiana Dunes than in the entire state of Hawaii.

Jack pine forest grows in dune valleys, which provide a habitat for other plants. The dunes are also home to junipers, goldenrod, beach heath, sand cherry and evening primrose. White-tailed deer sometimes shelter amid the dune valleys, and black bears occasionally pass through.

Forests

Much of the region, including the Great Lakes region and the Cuyahoga Valley, are home to second-growth forests. The regions were heavily logged from the 1800s onward and were nearly wiped out by the 1930s. Luckily a strong conservation movement has helped revitalize the forests over the last century.

Northern hardwood forests are among the most dominant across the Great Lakes. Here you'll find red maples, yellow birch, American beech and eastern hemlock as well as sugar maples – the source of maple syrup. These are the forests that draw autumn lovers in September and October, when the changing leaves transform the forests into a blaze of yellow, red and orange.

Further south, the southern Great Lakes forests stretch across much of Michigan's lower peninsula as well as a huge swath of Indiana and Ohio (including the Cuyahoga Valley). Agriculture and industry have diminished these once vast deciduous forests, which are dominated by oaks, elms, sugar maples and beech trees. Bogs, fens, river valleys and tall grass prairies add to the biodiversity of the region.

In the northern reaches of the Great Lakes and on islands, including Isle Royale, you find boreal forests more common to Canada. These conifer forests grow in cold, moist conditions, with common species like balsam fir, white spruce, mountain ash and aspen.

Pockets of old-growth forests survive, though you'll have to look hard to find them. Offshore of Sleeping Bear Dunes, South Manitou Island has the largest and oldest white cedars in Michigan. You'll find a stand of these towering northern trees on the southwest corner of the island in the aptly named grove of Valley of the Giants. The remote location and their proximity to dunes ultimately saved the trees from the axe. Windblown sand covering the bark led lumbermen to pass them by since sand can quickly dull the saws.

Over twice the size of the average white cedar, these Goliaths stand nearly 100ft tall and have trunks with diameters of 5ft. They are estimated to be 300 to 500 years old, though one fallen tree had 528 growth rings. Some visitors describe an almost mystical experience while walking through this extraordinarily rare forest.

The Badlands

History is literally written in the rocks in the Badlands. On a walk amid the striated canyons of South Dakota, you'll pass layers of history, each one representing a distinct geological period. The oldest layer is on the bottom, and successive layers have been added over millions of years, with the youngest layer on top. The Badlands owe their appearance to

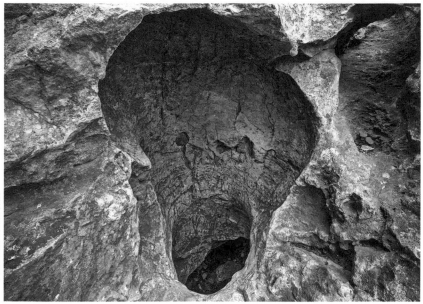

SERGE YATUNIN/GETTY IMAGES ©

Natural entrance to Wind Cave (p82)

the accumulation of sediments that turned to stone, followed by floods, rain and wind that shaped the canyons, buttes, mesas and hoodoos you see today.

If you visited 80 million years ago, you'd be walking on the bed of the Western Interior Seaway, a shallow inland sea that split the continent in two and stretched from the Arctic down to the Gulf of Mexico. Ancient marine life flourished in these warm waters, from oyster-like bivalves known as inoceramids to the fearsome 45ft marine reptile Mosasaurus. If you stood there for a spell (15 million or so years), you'd witness the upwelling of land, forcing the sea to drain north into the Arctic Ocean. Atop the dry shale lie the so-called yellow mounds, ancient fossilized soils that get their distinct color from a mineral called goethite.

The climate changed over the years, and by 35 million years ago it had become hot and humid, similar to the Everglades of today. Amid this jungle environment, new plant and animal species colonized the region, including alligators, aquatic turtles and brontotheres, a massive horned animal that's a relative of the rhinoceros. Fluvial mudstone, sand and siltstone from this period created the sedimentary layer called the Chadron Formation.

Over the next four million years, forest transformed into savannah with the arrival of a cooler, drier climate. Rivers carved their way through the plains, and now-extinct species of hog-like herbivores known as oreodonts grazed on the abundant grasses that grew here. They were hunted by saber-toothed cats and other big

Badlands Beyond the Park

Otherworldly rock formations known as badlands are formed by two fundamental forces: deposition (layers of rock gradually building up over the years) and erosion. Badlands stretch across parts of both North and South Dakota, though they can also be found in Montana, Nebraska and Wyoming. Other areas of the world also have badlands, including Canada, Taiwan, Argentina and New Zealand.

Subterranean Wonders

The national parks' caves are often overlooked by road-tripping families on summer vacations. After all, is walking around in a chilly, pitch-black tunnel really as appealing as spotting moose in the Boundary Waters or charging down sand dunes on shores of Lake Michigan? Maybe not on the surface, but the thrill of exploring the underworld's bizarre formations should not be overlooked. Amid the enormous cave systems of **Wind Cave**, rangers lead fascinating tours that bring geology to life. Sections of the cave are over 300 million years old, making it one of the oldest on the planet. Encompassing 154 miles of passages, Wind Cave is also one of the largest systems in the US (after Mammoth Cave, and another South Dakota standout, Jewel Cave).

predators. Periodic floods were followed by the appearance of more diverse varieties of oreodonts, as well as tiny deer-like protoceroas. The geological record of this time is preserved in the Brule Formation.

Drying, cooling conditions persisted from 25 million to 30 million years ago. Lying above the Brule Formation is the Sharps Formation, characterized by periodic volcanic eruptions in the Great Basin (across present-day Nevada and Utah), which covered this region in ash. This is the youngest formation of the park and consists of the peaks and pinnacles of the highest rocks in the Badlands.

Prairie

Early explorers passing through the area described it as a vast and featureless wasteland, yet despite the absence of forests and large bodies of water, these grasslands play a vital role in supporting diverse plant and animal life.

Prairies experience extreme fluctuations in temperature, which can vary by 140°F from the hottest to the coldest days. They also face regular storms that can bring an onslaught of rain, hail and snow, as well as the odd tornado and wildfire that can quickly engulf a region. Despite their devastating appearances, fires play a crucial role in the health of the grasslands. Without wildfires, non-native species of trees and shrubs would grow on the prairies, and over time the grasslands would transform into forests.

The essential life force of the prairie is grass, which comes in a variety of species depending on the region. These grasses have developed unique strategies for surviving in the harsh environment. More than half of the plants mass resides underground in their roots. This provides an essential food source during winter and droughts while also helping to build the soil and protect it from erosion. Long root systems extend down as much as 10ft to maximize the ability to reach water during dry periods. The growing parts of many plants reside underground so the grasses can survive wildfires and regrow after the flames have passed. Brightly colored flowers attract a variety of pollinators, including bees, butterflies, beetles and birds.

Deer, elk, bison, prairie dogs and other prairie animals rely on the grasslands for survival. Scores of bird species nest in the prairies or pass through on migratory routes each year. Predators big and small, from black-footed ferrets to long-horned owls and mountain lions, feed on the abundant animal life in the grasslands.

Prior to the arrival of Europeans, one third of the North American continent was covered by grasslands. Today only a fraction of it remains, with 99% of tall grass prairies and 75% of shortgrass prairies now gone. Originally home to millions of bison, you can get some sense of what parts of the prairie looked like in the Badlands, Theodore Roosevelt and Wind Cave, all in the Dakotas.

Behind the Scenes

Send Us Your Feedback

We love to hear from travelers – your comments keep us on our toes and help make our books better. Our well-traveled team reads every word on what you loved or loathed about this book. Although we cannot reply individually to your submissions, we always guarantee that your feedback goes straight to the appropriate authors, in time for the next edition. Each person who sends us information is thanked in the next edition.

Visit lonelyplanet.com/contact to submit your updates and suggestions or to ask for help. Our award-winning website also features inspirational travel stories and news.

Note: We may edit, reproduce and incorporate your comments in Lonely Planet products such as guidebooks, websites and digital products, so let us know if you are happy to have your name acknowledged. For a copy of our privacy policy visit lonelyplanet.com/legal.

Acknowledgements

Climate map data adapted from Peel MC, Finlayson BL & McMahon TA (2007) 'Updated World Map of the Köppen-Geiger Climate Classification', *Hydrology and Earth System Sciences*, 11, pp1633–44.

Cover: Badlands National Park, Larry Knupp/ Getty Images ©

This Book

This 1st edition of Lonely Planet's *Great Lakes and Midwest USA's National Parks* was researched and written by Regis St Louis, Anita Isalska and Brendan Sainsbury,

This guidebook was produced by the following:

Commissioning Editor Angela Tinson
Product Editors Gary Quinn, Jennifer McCann
Cartographer Rachel Imeson
Book Designer Carla Monitto
Cover Researcher Hannah Blackie
Thanks to Ronan Abayawickrema, Imogen Bannister, Kate Chapman, Melanie Dankel, Evan Godt, Victoria Harrison, Clare Healy, Sandie Kestell, Lyahna Spencer

Index

Our Story

A beat-up old car, a few dollars in the pocket and a sense of adventure. In 1972 that's all Tony and Maureen Wheeler needed for the trip of a lifetime – across Europe and Asia overland to Australia. It took several months, and at the end – broke but inspired – they sat at their kitchen table writing and stapling together their first travel guide, *Across Asia on the Cheap*. Within a week they'd sold 1500 copies. Lonely Planet was born.

Today, Lonely Planet has offices in the US, Ireland and China, with more than 2000 contributors. We share Tony's belief that 'a great guidebook should do three things: inform, educate and amuse'.

Our Writers

Regis St Louis

Regis grew up in a small town in the American Midwest and developed an early fascination with foreign dialects and world cultures. He spent his formative years learning Russian and a handful of Romance languages, which served him well on journeys across much of the globe. Regis has contributed to more than 50 Lonely Planet titles, covering destinations across six continents. Follow him @regisstlouis on Instagram and Twitter.

Anita Isalska

Anita is a travel journalist, editor and copywriter. After several merry years as a staff writer and editor, Anita now works freelance between Australia, the UK and any Alpine chalet with good wi-fi. Anita writes about France, Eastern Europe, Southeast Asia and off-beat travel. Read more on her website www.anitaisalska.com.

Brendan Sainsbury

Born and raised in the UK in a town that never merits a mention in any guidebook (Andover, Hampshire), Brendan spent the holidays of his youth caravanning in the English Lake District and didn't leave Blighty until he was 19. He's since squeezed 70 countries into a sometimes precarious existence as a writer and professional vagabond. In the last 11 years, he has written more than 40 books for Lonely Planet about places ranging from from Castro's Cuba to the canyons of Peru.

◄——————— More Writers ———————◄

STAY IN TOUCH LONELYPLANET.COM/CONTACT

IRELAND
Digital Depot, Digital Hub
Roe Lane (off Thomas St)
Dublin 8, D08 TCV4

USA
230 Franklin Rd, Building 2B
Franklin, TN 37064
☏ 615 988 9713

 twitter.com/ lonelyplanet

 facebook.com/ lonelyplanet

 instagram.com/ lonelyplanet

youtube.com/ lonelyplanet

 lonelyplanet.com newsletter